DOING IT NOW
IT CAN CHANGE YOUR LIFE.

Tested by Edwin C. Bliss's nationally held seminars on procrastination and time management, this 12-step program is quick, easy, and effective. You'll find your self-esteem growing and your attitudes changing as you progress through the book. *Doing It Now* will show you how to succeed in whatever goal you set for yourself—from cleaning out the closet to getting to the top of your profession. In short, it can change your life—and give you more free time to enjoy it!

12 SIMPLE STEPS TO
SELF-MASTERY AND SUCCESS

1. ADJUST YOUR ATTITUDE
2. DEVELOP A GAME PLAN
3. OVERCOME YOUR FEAR OF FAILURE
4. OVERCOME YOUR FEAR OF SUCCESS
5. RAISE YOUR ENERGY LEVEL
6. GET TOUGH WITH YOURSELF
7. ESTABLISH AN ACTION ENVIRONMENT
8. USE THE REINFORCEMENT PRINCIPLE
9. THE VALUE OF DELIBERATE DELAY
10. MANAGE YOUR TIME
11. USE VISIBLE REMINDERS
12. LEARN TO DEAL WITH THE
    TOP FORTY COP-OUTS

Bantam Books by Edwin C. Bliss

**GETTING THINGS DONE
DOING IT NOW**

DOING IT NOW

A Twelve-Step Program
for Curing Procrastination
and Achieving Your Goals

EDWIN C. BLISS

Illustrations by
Malcolm Hancock

BANTAM BOOKS
NEW YORK · TORONTO · LONDON · SYDNEY · AUCKLAND

DOING IT NOW

*A Bantam Book / published by arrangement with
Charles Scribner's Sons*

PRINTING HISTORY

Charles Scribner's edition published November 1983
A Writer's Digest Book Club Selection, January 1984
Serialized in Glamour *magazine, November 1983*

Bantam edition / October 1984
5 printings through August 1988

*Bantam Books are published by Bantam Books, a division of Bantam
Doubleday Dell Publishing Group, Inc. Its trademark, consisting of the
words "Bantam Books" and the portrayal of a rooster, is Registered in
U.S. Patent and Trademark Office and in other countries. Marca
Registrada. Bantam Books, 666 Fifth Avenue, New York, New York 10103.*

PRINTED IN THE UNITED STATES OF AMERICA

O   14   13   12   11   10   9   8   7

*This book is dedicated
to my son Bill,
who urged that it be written
. . . without delay*

Contents

We have left undone
those things
which we ought to have done . . .

THE BOOK OF COMMON PRAYER
1552

To the Reader

You may not know it, but you helped me write this book.

Well, not literally, of course; but you're represented as sort of a co-author. The book is in question-and-answer form, and I've tried, based on my experience in seminars and counseling, to let the questions represent those questions (and arguments) that I think you would present if you and I were sitting together talking (and arguing) about procrastination.

I hope I've done an adequate job responding to your questions. Vicariously or not, you've turned out to be a formidable antagonist!

But now I want to carry our joint venture a step further.

This time your role can be carried out only by you, and it will require your active, not vicarious, involvement.

In this book are to be found the tools that will enable you to overcome procrastination. But they won't work if you just read about them. My aim is not to increase your understanding of your problem, but to change your behavior, quite radically. For that to happen, it is essential that as you read you apply the principles to specific projects or tasks in your own life. And that can occur only if you have before you—in writing—a list of such projects.

So before you begin the first chapter I'd like you to put the book aside for a few minutes and make four lists:

1. List all of the things, large and small, that you are putting off in your place of work. The project you meant to begin, the suggestion you were going to make, the misunderstanding between you and your boss that you were going to resolve, the overdue report, the unfiled paperwork, the contacts you meant to follow up, the memo you were going to write. See if you can fill at least an entire page.

2. Now, make a separate list of tasks you've been putting off around your home, the household chores that have been nagging at you for weeks or months or maybe years. Take a tour of your yard, then go through your house room by room, attic to basement, and write down all the things you've been meaning to do "when I get the time."

3. Now make a third list, consisting of things you are postponing in the field of personal relationships. The letters or phone calls that have existed for so long as "intentions," the family reunion you've wanted to organize, the backpacking trip you've meant to take with your kids, the neighbor you've intended to get acquainted with, the phone call you should make to

your Aunt Mary, the school friendship you'd like to renew, the community action project you've been waiting for someone else to initiate.

4. And finally, make a list of the things you've been meaning to do for yourself some day. The art class you've wanted to take, the vacation you've postponed for too long, the bad habit you know you should extinguish, the exercise program you've intended to start, the language you'd like to learn.

Don't worry at this point about finding the time or the energy for all these things—we'll deal with that later. And don't worry about priorities. Just list all the things in each category that you should do, or would like to do, but which you have put off for some reason. Then, as you go through the book with those lists in front of you, you'll realize that I'm not talking about abstract concepts or hypothetical examples—I'm talking about you! And you'll relate the principles not to theoretical situations, but to the specific mental barriers preventing you from becoming the person you'd like to be.

Doing It
Now

Attitude Adjustment

Procrastination seems to be a universal fact of life. Shouldn't we just accept it as part of human nature and let it go at that?

Not at all. Some people do, of course, but they generally turn out to be the ones who are defeated by life.

But when something is so widespread, isn't it rather pointless to fight it?

No. Disease is widespread, but we don't shrug our shoulders and ignore it. The important thing is not how widespread a problem is but whether something can be done about it. And in the case of procrastination it can.

1

Are you sure? Where is the evidence that this problem can be overcome?

The evidence is found in the life of every successful human being. Successful people do not procrastinate—at least in matters relating to their field of achievement. It's as simple as that. Procrastination prevents success.

Wait a minute. Surely you can't mean that. Practically everybody admits to being a procrastinator. It's the common denominator of the human race.

Not really. It's the common denominator of people who fail to live up to their potential.

It's true that nearly everyone will jokingly admit to procrastination. But when successful people do so, what they are really saying is that there are some things that they would like to have done that they haven't done. That isn't the same thing as procrastination.

Maybe a definition would clarify things. Exactly what do you mean by procrastination?

I mean postponing something that you know in your heart should be done now instead of later. If you postpone a task in order to do something that really has greater importance and urgency, you can't accuse yourself of procrastination.

So what you're saying is that procrastination and justifiable delay are two different things.

Of course. And learning to distinguish between them is what this book is all about. That, and learning what to do when you catch yourself committing the sin of procrastination.

Did you say "sin"?

Yes.

Isn't that putting it a bit strongly? It's a bad habit, admittedly. Even a peccadillo, perhaps. But surely it can't be called a sin!

It certainly can. As any theologian will tell you, sin comes in two varieties. The sin of commission gets all the attention, but in the words of Ogden Nash,

It is the sin of omission, the second kind of sin,
That lays eggs under your skin.
The way you get really painfully bitten
Is by the insurance you haven't taken out and the checks
you haven't added up the stubs of and the appoint-
ments you haven't kept and the bills you haven't paid
and the letters you haven't written.
Also, about sins of omission there is one particularly pain-
ful lack of beauty,
Namely, it isn't as though it had been a riotous red letter
day or night every time you neglected to do your
duty;
You didn't get a wicked forbidden thrill
Every time you let a policy lapse or forgot to pay a bill;
You didn't slap the lads in the tavern on the back and
loudly cry, Whee,
Let's all fail to write just one more letter before we go
home, and this round of unwritten letters is on me.
No, you never get any fun
Out of the things you haven't done,
But they are the things that I do not like to be amid,
Because the suitable things you didn't do give you a lot
more trouble than the unsuitable things you did.[1]

In this matter of doing things when they should be done, I think that if we can become saints instead of sinners we will live happier, healthier, and more productive lives.

Okay, so procrastination is bad and we should all try to do something about it. But it still seems that with the innumerable problems besetting each of us, the question of whether we do something today or tomorrow is hardly a primary concern.

As a matter of fact, it is. So often it is the key to those other problems, large or small. Consider, for example, typical procrastinators whose problems are either created or intensified by delay:

- The compulsive drinker who resolves to contact Alcoholics Anonymous "the very next time I have a blackout."
- The worker who is going to confront the boss about that raise "when the time is right."
- The father who plans to spend some time with his kids "when work pressures aren't so great."
- The office manager who has some ideas that would increase efficiency, but who is waiting "until things settle down" to implement them.
- The salesman who postpones a call on a major prospect, fearing rejection because "the company hasn't had a good year."
- The woman who is going to stop smoking "as soon as I get pregnant."
- The high school student who is going to establish some good study habits "as soon as I get into college."
- The person who means to see the doctor about those chest pains, but decides "it would be a good idea to get caught up at the office first."
- The company that intends to begin a new research and development project "as soon as we can free someone to oversee the job."
- The nation that plans to balance its budget "as soon as things get better."

These people and institutions wouldn't see themselves as having much in common, but they share several things:

1. Each has a problem, whether large or small.
2. Each knows what should be done about the problem, and has determined to take a specific action. However—
3. Each is reluctant to take that action now, promising instead to act at some indeterminate time in the future.
4. Each makes performance of the task contingent upon something else. They will do it "as soon as . . ." or "when . . ." or "if . . ." This makes the delay seem temporary and justifiable. However, the contingency is usually just a convenient excuse instead of a legitimate reason for delay. What we have is a process of self-delusion.

All varieties of procrastination, in fact, involve self-delusion of one kind or another. They involve denial of reality, and refusal to weigh penalties and alternatives objectively.

In other words, you are saying that procrastination is stupid.

Exactly. It's a form of game-playing. And idiotic game-playing at that, because we ourselves are invariably the losers. In the words of the poet Robert Abrahams:

> *Some men die by shrapnel*
> *And some go down in flames,*
> *But most men perish inch by inch*
> *In play at little games.*[2]

Overcoming procrastination means giving up the games and being honest with ourselves.

5

You mentioned the varieties of procrastination. Isn't there just one variety—namely, putting things off?

No. There is one result, but there are a number of causes. I think the causes of procrastination can be grouped into four categories:

First are the *attitudinal* factors, which include such things as unwillingness to tolerate discomfort or unpleasantness, fear of failure, fear of success, low self-esteem, depression, boredom, shyness, and feelings of guilt.

Second are the *cognitive* blocks, such as inadequate information, unclear priorities, indecision, uncertainty about how to attack the problem and failure to appreciate the importance of timely action.

Third are *environmental* conditions or external factors that encourage delay. They include clutter, disorganization, noise, unmanageable workloads, diversionary activities, lack of needed tools, and friends or relatives who lure one from the chosen task.

And finally, there are the *physiological* barriers to timely action, including fatigue, stress, and illness.

Each instance of procrastination involves one or more of these. If you can pin down the cause of your procrastination, you will have taken a big step toward overcoming it and replacing it with the habit of prompt action. And then it won't be necessary for anyone ever to say of you:

> *He slept beneath the moon,*
> *He basked beneath the sun;*
> *He lived a life of going-to-do*
> *And died with nothing done.*[3]

So where does one begin the assault on procrastination?

One begins by discarding some untenable prejudices.

Such as?

Such as the belief that one is "just a born procrastinator," the assumption that we are dealing with an innate character defect that we are helpless to correct. We must stop excusing ourselves with the fallacious argument that we are the victims of genetic or environmental factors condemning us to the role of the legendary character who goes through life "a dollar short and a day late."

But isn't there considerable truth in this assumption— for some people, at least? Aren't all of us born with certain weaknesses? And if our weakness happens to be procrastination, shouldn't we accept it and just try to make the best of it? Why this compulsion to make ourselves over, instead of relaxing and enjoying life? What's wrong with the philosophy of the old song, "Que será, será, whatever will be, will be...."?

Que será, será is a lovely song, but a lousy philosophy. Nothing worthwhile was ever accomplished by anybody who met life with a shrug and an attitude of "whatever will be, will be." There are plenty of people who do choose that approach, of course, but they are the zombies. Instead of that motto, your slogan should be, *"Que quiero será"*— whatever *I* will, will be.

But surely you have heard such phrases as "Go with the flow," and "Don't push the river." Don't these admonitions suggest the wisdom of accepting what life has dished out to us and enjoying it instead of going on a binge of self-modification?

Not at all. Those phrases are perfectly valid in the proper context. It *is* foolish, of course, not to yield to the inevitable. But what is inevitable? One is reminded of the well-known Serenity Prayer by Dr. Reinhold Niebuhr:

> *O God, give us serenity to accept what cannot be changed,*
> *Courage to change what should be changed,*
> *And wisdom to distinguish the one from the other.*

This book is based on the belief that as far as our own behavior is concerned, when we achieve the wisdom spoken of in that prayer, most of us will emphasize the courage part more and the serenity part less.

Life is not a situation, but a process; not static, but dynamic. Its essential element is change, and the great question facing each of us is whether we will channel that change in the directions we want to go, shaping our destiny, or whether we will permit our activities and our character to be determined by those random forces we call fate. To the extent that we procrastinate, we are following the second course.

But this all sounds like such a chore! To fight procrastination—along with all the other imperfections we all have in our makeup—seems like a never-ending process. It seems as if you are asking people to be constantly at war with themselves.

In a sense that is true. The concept of an eternal struggle within us, between good and evil, between self-mastery and self-indulgence, goes back to the Garden of Eden; it is the great theme running through life and literature. But the testament of the human race is that the battle is worth fighting, that it gives zest to life, and that victory is sweet. In the words of the Roman poet Publius Syrus, "The greatest victory is victory over self; to be conquered by self is of all things the most shameful and vile."

Yes, it is a battle. But it can be a very satisfying one, if one is on the offensive and winning victories. Remember, when one begins to win, subsequent victories become easier, as the enemy weakens. Our strength and ability to overcome procrastination grow each time we chalk up a triumph, however small.

One of the notable achievers of recent years is Ray Kroc, chairman of the board of McDonald's, the man who parlayed the humble hamburger into a fortune. He says, "The longer I live, the more importance I attach to a man's ability to manage and discipline himself. . . . The man with the capacity for self-discipline can tell himself to do the truly important things first. Therefore, if there is not enough time to go around and something must be neglected, it will be the less essential task.

"Here is the most interesting thing about the capacity for self-discipline. He who wants it may have it! . . . The one ingredient we most need for success is ours for the asking, for the wanting, if we only want it enough!"[4]

Self-discipline. That's where it all starts. There's no substitute.

In his book *Excellence*, John Gardner, founder of Common Cause, put it this way: "Some people may have greatness thrust upon them. Very few have excellence thrust upon them. They achieve it. They do not achieve it unwittingly, by 'doin' what comes naturally'; and they don't stumble into it in the course of amusing themselves. All excellence involves discipline and tenacity of purpose."[5]

But you can't just turn it on. Suppose you lack this attribute that is supposed to be so essential. How do you develop it?

For starters, you change your attitude toward difficult tasks, and admit to yourself that postponing them will not make them easier. Tell yourself that from now on you are never going to put anything on the back burner without running the rationalization through your mental computer for careful analysis. As you weigh the reasons methodically and objectively, you will begin to spend less of your time in the fantasy world of the procrastinator and more in the real world, where the penalties of postponement are recognized as unacceptable.

And you start also with something even more basic: an attitude of affirmation. You must tell yourself that you really *can* change, if you want to. The tendency to procrastinate isn't something one is born with, like color blindness. It's a habit, and you can alter habits. The way you begin is by admitting that you can, and resolving that you will.

This "attitude of affirmation" you speak of—isn't that just another term for "the power of positive thinking"? And isn't that pretty old stuff?

The answer to both questions is yes.

Norman Vincent Peale calls it *positive thinking*. Robert Schuller uses the term *possibility thinking*. Clement Stone talks about PMA—positive mental attitude. Maxwell Maltz coined the term *psycho-cybernetics*. Wayne Dyer speaks of becoming a no-limit person. An earlier proponent of positive thinking, Jesus of Nazareth, put it this way: "According to your faith be it unto you."

So it's nothing new. But one of the ironies of the human condition is that old verities are suspect. A truth that has been proved millions of times through the ages will be questioned because of its very antiquity. We have to learn it all over again, sometimes dressing it up in new garb. Thus each generation and each individual has to be convinced anew that love is better than hate, that peace is better than war, that virtue is better than vice . . . and that positive thinking brings success and negative thinking produces failure.

Sophisticates may scoff at what they describe as the simplistic message of a Robert Schuller, but even they are awed by the magnificence of the great Crystal Cathedral in Garden Grove, California, which "possibility thinking" has produced. Even more important, they must be impressed by the changes that have occurred in countless lives because of the "simplistic" message of affirmation.

In the words of Dr. Karl Menninger, the famous psychiatrist, "Attitudes are more important than facts." Those six words express a profound truth. Change your attitude toward procrastination and you will have taken a major step toward overcoming it.

But to change your attitude by a mere act of will seems impossible. It's like lifting yourself by your bootstraps. If you don't honestly believe you can overcome procrastination, how do you trick yourself into believing you can? How do you convince yourself of something that simply isn't so?

You don't. Because it *is* so! You aren't tricking yourself, or lying to yourself—you are stating a truth.

And remember, we are not talking here about just procrastination but about the things you are procrastinating *on*. The skill you want to develop, the weight loss you would like to achieve, the language you would like to learn, the house you would like to build—all of these things are attainable once you get it through your head that they really are, and that the only thing blocking them is your own negativism: your refusal to believe in your own capacity and then to act on that belief.

Okay, so let's grant that faith in yourself is a big plus; the fact still remains that sometimes your faith may not be justified. People can't do things beyond their powers, and they know it. In such a situation how can they engage

11

in "possibility thinking"? You are asking people to close their eyes to reality.

Not at all. You see, there is little danger of people setting goals for themselves that are truly beyond their reach. It does happen, but very rarely. For example, I might fantasize about myself as a great movie star, or as world heavyweight boxing champion, or as the world's greatest detective, but I would never set those things as goals. Knowing that I don't have the required attributes, and knowing that my interests lie in other directions, I would never commit myself to them.

No, the problem isn't in setting goals that are too high; the problem is setting goals that are too low. And most of us do. Consequently, we achieve only a portion of what we could.

What portion?

It's anybody's guess. But the great psychologist-philosopher William James[6] estimated that most people use only about one-tenth of their potential powers. He said, "Everyone knows that on any given day there are energies slumbering in him which the incitements of that day do not call forth. Compared with what we ought to be, we are only half awake. Our fires are damped, our drafts are checked. We are making use of only a small part of our possible mental and physical resources."*

But how does all this relate to procrastination?

When "our fires are damped," and we use only part of our potential, procrastination is nearly always a factor.

---

* A modern-day philosopher, Linus (alias Charles M. Schulz), put it more succinctly: "Life is like a ten-speed bicycle. Most of us have gears that we never use!"

Shyness, laziness, indecision, indifference, fear, negative thinking, dissipation, fuzzy goals, poor self-image—these and many other things can put a ceiling on our level of achievement. *But the mechanism through which these inhibitors manifest themselves is usually procrastination.* Our shyness, laziness, indecision, fear, or whatever causes us to postpone doing the things we know we should do, and the result is failure, total or partial. As someone has said, "People don't fail because they intend to fail. They fail because they fail to do what they intend to do."

So you're saying, then, that procrastination is not so much a disease as a symptom.

Exactly.

In that case, shouldn't we be concerning ourselves with the causes rather than with the effect? Shouldn't we be figuring out what to do about shyness, laziness, indecision, fear, etc., rather than dealing with the procrastination that results from these problems?

We're going to do both. Obviously, if we can identify and eliminate the causes that's the way to go. But behavioral scientists have shown that the reverse procedure also works— even better, in many cases. Changing an undesired behavior can alter the attitudes that caused the behavior in the first place.

For example?

Suppose you feel depressed, so you frown and act grumpy. Suddenly you are put in a situation requiring you to smile and be pleasant. You find your depression diminishes, and soon you are smiling not because you are forcing yourself to but because you feel more cheerful. The change in behavior has caused a change in attitude.

How does this apply to procrastination?

Suppose, for example, you are tempted to put off the writing of a difficult letter of apology. If you can somehow force yourself to write it anyway—and before you are compelled to—your attitude changes. It still may be an unpleasant task, but you get a sense of self-satisfaction from having tackled a tough chore promptly. Your self-esteem goes up a notch. The next time you are tempted to procrastinate on an unpleasant but necessary task you are a little less likely to succumb to the temptation.

So we are going to consider not only how we can change our attitudes toward procrastination, but how we can change our behavior *despite* our attitudes. If we attack the problem from both ends, we increase our chance of success.

The first step is to change the way we think about procrastination itself. We must recognize it for the evil it is. We must think of it not as a trifling weakness to be brushed off with a joke but as a malignant tumor on our psyche, which must be excised if we are ever to become the person we would like to be.

It would be no exaggeration to say that for millions of people the tendency to procrastinate is the primary reason for their failure to achieve a rich, fulfilling life. So instead of saying to ourselves, "This is a weakness I happen to have, and I guess I'm stuck with it," we must say, "This is the culprit responsible for putting a ceiling on my achievement. It is a deeply ingrained habit—but it is *only* a habit, and habits can be changed. I can lick this thing, and, so help me God, I will."

When you begin talking to yourself like that you are on the threshold of a new era in your life. Until you make that commitment, you are destined to continue sputtering along at a fraction of your potential.

The choice is yours. Which will it be?

Taking the First Step

I'm going to ask you now to put yourself in one of two categories.

On page xiv you were asked to stop reading long enough to make four lists. Did you?

If you did, you're in Category 1, which means that you've already made a sound start toward solving your problem. Give yourself a pat on the back. You may skip the rest of this little lecture and proceed to the next chapter.

If you didn't follow those instructions, you're in Category 2, and it's time we had a little talk.

Why didn't you make those lists? Chances are, you made a mental note to do it—but later. You thought you would finish reading the book, and then, if you were in the mood, and if you were not busy with something else, and if you were convinced it was worth the bother, you would go back and make those four lists.

You know the word that describes your behavior, don't you? Procrastination!

Look: The reason you are reading this book is that you realize procrastination is a problem in your life, and you've decided to see whether something can be done about it. Well, the first thing to recognize is that we are dealing with a behavioral problem, not an intellectual one. Your goal is not to gain insight, or to amuse yourself for a few hours, or to experience the "Aha!" effect. Your goal is to wrench some bad habits loose from their moorings and substitute some good ones. That doesn't happen just from reading a book. It happens if and only if you change your attitude toward procrastination, and resolve to expend whatever effort is required to lick it.

So before going on to the next chapter go back and reread page xiv. Then put down the book and make your lists, and we'll be on our way.

Now!

Step 2

Develop a Game Plan

A positive attitude about overcoming procrastination is fine, but it doesn't solve the problem. Let's get down to the nuts and bolts. Exactly how does a person translate that positive attitude into reality?

First, you must stop thinking in generalities, and focus your attention on one specific task. Then the problem is not "How do I stop procrastinating?" but "How do I make myself start painting the house?" You can't get a handle on a generality; a specific problem you can deal with.

Having selected the behavior you want to correct, the

17

next step is to analyze the problem and decide what's causing the delay. Such varied causes as fatigue, lack of information, fear of failure, distraction, shyness, conflicting priorities, and so on, obviously will all require different approaches. *In most cases, willpower alone won't do the job!*

People have a tendency, however, not to look for the "why," or not to look deeply enough. In other words, they procrastinate on analyzing the reasons for their procrastination! Unconsciously, they recognize that focusing attention on the cause of a problem is the first step toward solving it, and they quail at the thought that they might be about to take that fateful first step.

Why do you say that? If a person sincerely wants to solve a problem, and knows what should be done to solve it, it would be illogical not to take the necessary steps.

True, but who said people behave logically?* Most don't, which is the reason for books like this one. Somehow we must counteract that streak of masochism that causes us to close our eyes to the real reasons for our procrastination.

So try to *categorize* your problem, and clarify what it is that has been causing you to procrastinate. And remember, no generalities, no lame excuses such as, "I just have a habit of putting things off." Ask such questions as, "Honestly, what's my problem? Indecision? Shyness? Boredom? Inability to tolerate unpleasantness? Lack of needed tools? Ignorance? Disorganization? Fear? Fatigue? Is there any one word or phrase that sums up why I haven't been able to get this particular task under way?"

I call this process Pigeonholing, because it is an effort to put your problem into a very specific category, zeroing in on the cause rather than the excuse. When you attach an

---

* As someone has observed, if we really lived in a logical world, it would have been the men rather than the women who rode sidesaddle.

accurate label to a problem, the solution frequently becomes self-evident.

For example, if you establish that indecision is the cause of your problem, you have put your finger on the solution and you are likely to sit down and make some decisions. If you put your problem in the mental pigeonhole marked "Inadequate Information," you'll start looking for the additional data you need. If you recognize that your procrastination is caused by fatigue, fear, poor self-image, environmental problems, poor time management, etc., you may turn to the section of this book that discusses those factors, and perhaps you'll gain some helpful insights.

The first step is to find the right pigeonhole. Put the real reason for your delay into words. The precise statement of any problem is the most important step in its solution.

In the search for causes, however, be careful not to mistake excuses for reasons.

What do you mean by that?

Don't let yourself get away with such cop-outs as, "I just haven't been able to find the time," or "There aren't enough hours in the day," or "Things keep coming up." Dig a little deeper. Face up to the *real* "why," not the rationalization. Be honest with yourself.

But the reason for delay is often none of the things you've mentioned. It may just be that the job is overwhelming. For example, suppose you would like to design and build your own house. However, you realize that there will be countless difficulties with financing, zoning, utilities, style, materials, location, contracting, subcontracting, landscaping, etc., and the whole undertaking seems mindboggling. And since a boggled mind isn't conducive to action, your dream house remains just a dream. How do you cope with this?

19

One way is what I call the Salami Technique.

Whenever a task seems overwhelming, pause for a moment and do a little thinking on paper. List chronologically every step that must be taken to complete the job. The smaller the steps, the better—even little mini-tasks that will take only a minute or two should be listed separately.

I call this the Salami Technique because it seems to me that contemplation of an overwhelming task is like looking at a large uncut salami: it's a huge, crusty, greasy, unappetizing chunk; you don't feel you can get your teeth into it. But when you cut it into thin slices you transform it into something quite different. Those thin slices are inviting; they make your mouth water, and after you've sampled one slice you tend to reach for another. Cutting up your overwhelming task into tiny segments can have the same effect. Now, instead of looking at a gargantuan project, you're looking at a series of tiny tasks, each of which, considered separately, is manageable. And you begin to realize that they will indeed be considered separately.

The Chinese philosopher Lao Tzu's maxim that a journey of a thousand miles must begin with a single step doesn't really help us much until we know precisely in which direction we want to travel. With our list in front of us, we have a concrete idea of what that first step will be, and also the second, and the third. We have a road map that will guide us to our destination. Since each step completed leads logically to the next, we quickly establish momentum, and the job is under way.

It all sounds so simple. And, if you'll forgive a candid observation, it seems rather elementary. Don't most people do something like this? Does anyone ever build a house, for example, without making lists?

Of course not. But too often our dreams wind up in limbo without the list even being made. Or a list is made, but it isn't the kind we're talking about. A meticulously prepared step-by-step list of small tasks that need to be done —not just a random jotting down of a bunch of major things to do—seals the commitment, provides a blueprint for action, and triggers that action. But to be effective it must be chronological and it must be detailed. It must be a compilation of "instant tasks," so that you are dealing with salami slices, not a salami.

Remember that while this approach is especially helpful in getting started on overwhelming tasks, it also works with smaller ones that don't really seem to call for a sequential outline of actions.

For example, suppose you want to make a certain suggestion to your boss, but find yourself putting it off because you are afraid it will be rejected. It may seem that what is indicated is a simple one-step action—just go in and make your suggestion, and see what happens. And if you can make yourself do so, of course, that's the way to go. But if you find yourself procrastinating, try breaking that one-step action down *on paper* into tiny increments. Your "salami slices" might look like this:

1. Check file to refresh memory of pertinent facts.
2. Outline presentation.
3. Mentally rehearse presentation.
4. Identify possible objections.
5. Determine response to each objection.
6. Arrange time for presentation.
7. Make presentation.

But those are the steps one would naturally take anyway, aren't they?

Of course. You're not doing anything you wouldn't do anyway, except for one thing: the actual writing of the list.

Making a sequential list is an easy thing to do. And once it exists it acts as sort of a detonator, launching you into the task you were putting off.

It also serves another purpose. If you are interrupted during the performance of the task, you will know precisely where to pick up when you return. Without a written list, you often experience a mental block about resuming the activity. You've forgotten just where you were and what was to come next.

Properly used, a pencil can be one of the most effective weapons in the battle against procrastination.

Couldn't this process turn into a way of avoiding action? If instead of just going ahead and doing the job, one sits down and makes a detailed list of all the steps involved, doesn't that constitute delay? You seem to be encouraging—of all things—procrastination!

Not at all. What I am encouraging is an orderly approach. One of the principles of management is that, to be effective, planning must be separated from execution. Failure to do this generally results in poor results in both functions.

A good example of this is in the planning of a day. In the study of time management, we have found that scheduling the day early in the morning is not nearly as effective as doing it the preceding afternoon. In other words, the best time to plan Tuesday's activities is not the first thing Tuesday morning, but the last thing Monday, before leaving work. If you do your planning on Tuesday morning, you are planning under pressure: the day is under way, the phone is ringing, there are insistent matters clamoring to be taken care of. Your inclination is to roll up your sleeves and start doing things, instead of calmly and objectively analyzing *which* things you should be doing. And the things you are most inclined to begin doing often are not the top priority ones. You begin spinning your wheels. The important task that can be postponed tends to be postponed because of our compulsion to skip the planning and get the day started by doing something—"getting busy"—instead of acting out of long-term considerations.

If you plan Tuesday's work on Monday afternoon, however, you are in quite a different mood. Knowing that whatever you plan doesn't have to be done *now*, you are more objective. You assign yourself the tough tasks, knowing that a good night's sleep stands between you and the execution of the chore. You feel almost as if you were planning for someone else, and the tendency to postpone tasks until some vague future time is diminished.

This principle applies not just in planning a day, but in any kind of planning. Treat *planning* and *doing* as separate and distinct aspects of the job. One way to accomplish this is to plan, on paper, what you intend to do before even getting started—provided the task is a complex one, or one you are tempted to put off.

But suppose for some reason—laziness, time pressure, or simply because it doesn't seem worth the bother—a person doesn't want to take the trouble to write out a sequential list but is still bothered by the specter of procrastination. Any alternative suggestions?

Yes. Instead of the systematic assault on the task we've been talking about, another approach is just to make yourself do something—anything—in connection with it. I call this the Leading Task. It has also been referred to as the "Swiss Cheese Method," the idea being that you poke holes in the task until it resembles a Swiss cheese. Another writer calls it the "nibbling" approach (writers in this field seem to have hors d'oeuvres on their mind). Others call it the "bits and pieces" approach, the "start-up task," or the "baby step method."

Suppose you are putting off writing a letter. Instead of

23

trying to force yourself to write it (you've already tried that and it didn't work), just make yourself take one small step, with the understanding that after having done so you will decide then whether or not to proceed. That one step might be looking up the address, or rolling a piece of paper into the typewriter, or getting out the file, or writing down the three points you want to mention—anything, just so it's an overt action, something physical. It's a way of breaking the psychological logjam, and it's based, of course, on the fact that things at rest tend to remain at rest, while things in motion tend to remain in motion. Newton's laws apply in human behavior as well as in physics.

But some undertakings don't lend themselves to being broken down into smaller tasks. For example, suppose you should tackle a big backlog of filing that has accumulated, and it will take about an hour. There isn't any convenient way to break that kind of job down into "instant tasks."

In that case you may want to try the Five-Minute Plan. Make a deal with yourself, as in the preceding example, only this time instead of promising to do one segment, promise yourself that you will work on the task for five minutes. At the end of that time, you are free to turn to something else, if desired, or you may decide to spend another five minutes. No matter how distasteful the task, you can usually talk yourself into committing a mere five minutes to it.

Some people find this method works best with a timer. Set your timer for five minutes and resolve to see how much you can accomplish before it sounds.

At the end of the five minutes, if you don't feel like continuing, don't. A deal is a deal. But before setting the task aside, jot down a time when you will invest another five minutes.

This procedure is similar to the one followed by Alcoholics Anonymous. They have found that most alcoholics are discouraged when they think of promising never to take another drink; they can't commit themselves to such a seemingly unattainable goal. So they are encouraged instead to make a commitment to stay on the wagon for just a short period. Anybody can resist temptation for just five minutes. When they've done so, they try for another five, and this time it's a little easier, because they've demonstrated to themselves that they can set a modest goal and successfully meet it. Gradually they begin thinking in increments of a day or a week, and then they're well on their way to sobriety.

It works. Try it right now. Select one of the tasks you've been putting off, then lay the book aside, set the timer for five minutes, and commit yourself to work on that task intensively to see what you can do in that time. Try racing against the clock by going all out during that period, the way a sprinter does in a race. On your mark . . . get set . . . GO!

That wasn't so hard, was it? And don't you feel good about yourself right now? Wasn't it an exhilarating feeling to plunge into that obnoxious task you've been avoiding for so long? And didn't you feel an urge to continue while you had some momentum? (If you did, I hope you gave in to it.) The smugness you feel right now can be yours any time you want it. So indulge yourself—give yourself a small achievement to gloat over. Frequently.

In order to get the momentum you speak of, is it always a good idea to "ease in" to a task, doing the simplest and most pleasant part first?

Usually it is, but sometimes the exact opposite works. Sometimes it pays to identify the most difficult part and take care of it first. I call this the Worst First approach.

25

That doesn't make sense. You can't have it both ways. If one way works, the other one shouldn't.

Actually, there are three ways of reacting when you are confronted with a complex task. One way is to get your foot in the door by doing the easiest part first and building some momentum. The second is to tackle the hardest part first and get the smug feeling that comes from getting something unpleasant out of the way as soon as possible (the old idea of eating your spinach first and your strawberry shortcake second). The third way—the way of the procrastinator—is to do neither, just leaving the task in limbo because it is unpleasant and because instead of choosing either of those plans of action you've chosen a plan of avoidance.

Would you give an example of what you're talking about?

Sure. Suppose you have a group of volunteers, each of whom is supposed to call a list of people for donations to a political campaign. This is the kind of task most people find distasteful.

Some in the group will find it easiest to begin by contacting the most likely contributors—the good friends of the candidate—first. Then, warmed by the positive reception they are likely to get, they will feel less reluctant about calling those prospects on the list who are more likely to be grumpy, tightfisted and obnoxious.

Others in the group (and many experienced salespeople will choose this approach) will find it preferable to select the grumpiest person on the list and make that call first. When it is completed they can say, "I've got that S.O.B. out of the way; from here on it will be a breeze!"

Either system will work; it's a matter of individual style and, of course, the nature of the task. In either case you have made a commitment, you have adopted a definite game plan. What will *not* work is the third alternative, which is to postpone the chore until tomorrow in the hope that by some inexplicable miracle it will then become easier.

We're building up quite an armamentarium of techniques: so far we have Pigeonholing, the Salami Technique, the Leading Task, and the Five-Minute Plan. Are there others?

Yes, indeed. One is the Balance Sheet Method.

Select some task you've been putting off. Now take a sheet of paper, and on the left side of the page list the reasons you are procrastinating. On the right side of the page list the benefits of getting the job done. Now compare the two lists. Generally you'll find the reasons for procrastinating so insipid, and the reasons for action so compelling, that you become disgusted with your indolence and swing into action.

But doing it on paper is the secret. Excuses that seem quite adequate when they have not been clearly enunciated are exposed for the frauds they really are when reduced to writing.

Of course, sometimes the reasons for postponement may, on examination, be found to be quite valid, in which case you won't need to feel guilty about procrastination. The Balance Sheet Method, in other words, can be an excellent tool in reaching sound decisions about whether or not to take a certain course of action.

Benjamin Franklin often prepared a Balance Sheet when faced with a difficult decision. He wrote:

> . . . all the reasons pro and con are not present to the mind
> at the same time; but sometimes one set present themselves
> and at other times another, the first being out of sight. To
> get over this, my way is to divide half a sheet of paper by
> a line into two columns; writing over the one "Pro" and

over the other "Con." Then during three or four days' consideration I put down under the different heads short hints of the different motives that at different times occur to me for and against the measure. When I have thus got them all together in one view I endeavor to estimate their respective weights; and where I find two, one on each side, that seem equal I strike them both out. If I find a reason pro equal to some two reasons con, I strike out the three. If I judge some two reasons con equal to some three reasons pro I strike out the five; and thus proceeding I find at length where the balance lies . . . and come to a determination accordingly. And, though the weight of reasons cannot be taken with the precision of algebraic quantities, yet when each is thus considered separately and comparatively and the whole lies before me, I think I can judge better and am less liable to make a rash step; and in fact I have found great advantage from this kind of equation in what may be called moral or prudential algebra.[1]

This weighing of alternatives is what we will do every time we approach a decision; the only "new" element is doing it on paper. And if Benjamin Franklin, one of the great achievers of all time, found it worth his time to reduce the pros and cons to writing, perhaps we all could benefit from such a practice.

There is an alternative to the Balance Sheet Method that works even better for many people. Instead of making a pro and con list, you simply sit down and write out your feelings about the thing you are postponing. Talk to yourself on paper. Since you are writing only for yourself, don't worry about syntax and don't pull any punches. How do you really feel about the task? How do you feel about yourself for postponing it? What constructive steps might you take to get the show on the road? What, exactly, do you intend to do? When?

This may be done as an isolated exercise, or it can be one aspect of keeping a journal. Many psychiatrists and psychologists are taking renewed interest in the power of a journal to cause behavior change.

Wait a minute. Are you recommending keeping a diary?

Not in the sense of making a daily record of your experiences. Most of us have little need to know what we did on Tuesday, April 7th. The kind of journal I'm speaking of is primarily a record of thoughts and feelings, rather than just activities. It's a great way of getting your act together— clarifying goals, analyzing motives, planning corrective action, reinforcing desired behavior, getting to know and like yourself better, and thereby changing your attitudes.

The noted psychiatrist Ira Progoff is a leading advocate of this method. He recommends a rather structured document, which he calls the "Intensive Journal," with sections for such things as Stepping Stones, Intersections (Roads Taken and Not Taken), Life History Log (Recapitulations and Rememberings), Inner Wisdom Dialogue, and sections for writing about your relationships with other people, your feelings about situations and circumstances, and so on. In response to the question, "How often should I make my entries in the Intensive Journal?" he says:

> There are no fixed rules or requirements. The purpose of the Intensive Journal is not to give us one more thing to feel guilty about not doing. We already have enough of that, and enough regulations for our life. But the purpose of working with the Journal is to give ourselves the means and freedom of expressing the inner process of our lives when it wells up in us and desires expression. Writing your entries in your Intensive Journal

should not be a chore. Once you have established a dialogue relationship with your Journal, your inner self will tell you when there are things to be written and it will become natural for you to do so. Recording Journal entries when they are there to be written will become an accepted part of your life.[2]

I have tried and benefited from all of the techniques I discuss in this book, but I've found this one especially helpful, not just in confronting procrastination, but in dealing with life in general. When things seem to be getting muddled I roll a sheet of paper into my typewriter and type, with no concern for grammar, punctuation, style, or cohesion. The resulting mishmash is something that would make little sense to other people, I'm sure, but I find it most helpful. I file my sheets in a looseleaf binder, and months or years later I am fascinated as I review the musings of an earlier time. I may find a particular entry encouraging, stimulating, thought-provoking, amusing, naive, illogical, or just plain boring, but at least I have the benefit of a different perspective, removed from the pressures of the present moment. I find that it helps me to see the forest instead of just the trees, and that it has a catalytic effect.

As you read this book you will recognize that many of the points apply to specific habits you have developed, and you may make a mental note to make certain changes. But don't let it go at that—mental notes are easily misplaced. You can intensify and preserve your insights and intentions by recording them in a journal.

Are there any negative effects connected with keeping a journal?

Yes, in some cases. Sometimes a journal will degenerate into nothing more than a confession of inadequacies, a *mea culpa* chronicling shortcomings, in which case it may be a downer, just reaffirming your guilt feelings. Or it may have a cathartic effect, as confession sometimes does, making you feel better—but without stimulating you to *do* better. These things won't happen if, in being honest with yourself, you will be honest about your achievements and your admirable qualities, as well as your failures and your weaknesses. And your time focus is important, too: write not just about where you are and how you got there, but about where you're headed and how you'll get there. To forestall the tendency to procrastinate, direct most of your attention to the things you can do right now to make the future more rewarding.

Is there any example of this journal technique that you would recommend as a model?

You don't need a model. Develop your own approach instead of trying to conform to someone else's format. However, if you want to see how one man four centuries ago turned this process of written self-examination into an art form, read *The Essays* of Michel de Montaigne. (Be sure to get the Donald Frame translation.[3])

And if the word "journal" turns you off, just sit right down and write yourself a letter. It amounts to about the same thing.

You realize, surely, that writing is an ordeal for most people and that most of your readers aren't likely to follow your advice, however sound it may be. For those who have a mental block about writing, what do you recommend?

I recommend talking to yourself.

Of course you mean that figuratively, not literally, don't you?

No, I mean it literally. When you find yourself repeatedly postponing something you know you should do, go to a

31

private room and talk to yourself out loud as if you were the proverbial Dutch uncle.* Be blunt, direct, honest. Ask yourself what the hell is going on, and why you have failed to do things that you know damn well should be done. But don't just make it an exercise in self-flagellation: your message is not "I am a slob," or "I am a no-good procrastinator." Instead, it should be along the lines of, "This continuing procrastination is unacceptable, and it's going to end immediately. Here is what I am going to do to get started. . . ."

Tell yourself what you are *going* to do, not what you *should* do. Commit yourself to a specific action at a specific time. Make it a pep talk: assure yourself that you can do it. End on a positive note.

Honestly now, isn't this a bit weird? If people find out you're talking to yourself won't they wonder if you're playing with a full deck?

Perhaps. But if it works, who cares? As a matter of fact, this is a tried and true method of self-motivation. Many athletes have learned that talking to themselves before a contest can help to get them psyched up so they are "itchin' for action."

But that's because their purpose is to get the adrenalin flowing. It may work for a person who's about to engage in physical competition, such as a boxing or tennis match, but does that mean that it's equally effective in getting psyched up for doing chores?

Why not? As a matter of fact, researchers have found that talking to yourself can be an excellent way of changing

---

* Some people find it helpful to talk to themselves in a mirror. Jack Dempsey often used this technique prior to a fight.

attitudes, building self-control, and clarifying priorities—all of which diminish the temptation to procrastinate. Impulsive children can be taught to control their behavior by simply telling themselves out loud to slow down.[4]

The mind tends to respond positively to affirmations and verbal commands, even though they originate not from someone in a position of authority but from the mind itself. Just as you can program a computer, you can program yourself. But, as with the computer, the programming must not be ambiguous: it must be specific, concrete, and categorical.

Of course, talking out loud isn't always necessary. If you can accomplish the same thing with a mental admonition, fine. But when that doesn't work, consider intensifying the input by getting your voice and your ears into the act.

Aristotle Onassis talked to himself when faced with difficult problems, or when preparing himself for an important presentation. And it was not idle mumbling, such as we associate with senility—it was a crisp, clear, animated, uninhibited performance. In his book *The Fabulous Onassis*, Christian Cafarkis says:

> I discovered the truth of this "legend" one night in Monte Carlo soon after one of our cruises with the Churchills.
> Around eleven o'clock I was on deck smoking a final cigarette before going to bed. All of a sudden Onassis appeared on the main deck below, walking with his hands behind his back, talking, then stopping from time to time before going on again. I could hear his voice only intermittently because of the gusts of wind that evening, but I definitely thought he was with someone I simply couldn't see; the enormous smokestack blocked my view. But when he finally reached the bow, there was no longer any doubt: he was speaking to himself in Greek.
> That night I made a great discovery, perhaps even

learned a secret of this man's success. I saw Onassis spend two solid hours asking himself out loud all the questions that he might have to answer before going to a particular meeting or appointment.[5]

Another billionaire who soliloquized when he felt a need to reinforce his good intentions was John D. Rockefeller. "Your future hangs on every day that passes," he told himself repeatedly during the critical, chaotic period when Standard Oil was beginning to take shape. "Look out or you will lose your head—go steady."

So the concept of clarifying and reinforcing intentions by verbalizing them is nothing new. Several decades ago Dale Carnegie urged that this be done as part of a daily routine. He said, "Is giving yourself a pep talk every day silly, superficial, childish? No—on the contrary. It is the very essence of sound psychology."[6]

I don't know that I would go so far as to recommend a daily pep talk, but I do think that perhaps once or twice a year, if we feel that life is slipping through our fingers, it might be appropriate to take ourselves to the woodshed.

Since Dale Carnegie's time, incidentally, technology has blessed us with something that can add a new dimension to this process.

What is that?

The cassette recorder.

Just talking to yourself can have a powerful effect, but some people get even more benefit from a self-lecture if they record it. Then, whenever they are tempted to goof off, they can just play back what they said when they were in a more buoyant mood, thus getting the needed shot in the arm—or kick in the rear, as the case may be.

Besides being a reusable medium for self-motivation,

the cassette recorder has another advantage: some people find they simply *can't* talk to themselves out loud as we've discussed—they feel self-conscious when pacing the floor soliloquizing, Hamlet-style. But with the recorder they are, in effect, dictating a memo to themselves, making the process more acceptable.

I have done this on a number of occasions. I usually carry a cassette recorder on trips, so that I can dictate letters or memos following a meeting or a seminar. Sometimes instead of dictating something to be typed, I will make a tape for my own use only, reminding myself of things I've been putting off, mistakes I've made, or principles to be remembered. I tend to be rather scathing on such occasions, and sometimes I wince when I hear the tape later, but I find it gives an objectivity to my thoughts that nothing else can.

And the beautiful thing about the recorder, when used this way, is that it has no "down" moods. No matter how discouraged, frustrated, or stress-ridden you may be at a later time, a flick of the button will give you an upbeat analysis of your problem, a positive admonition about what needs to be done, and a firm reassurance that you can and will do it. It's a form of packaged encouragement, tailor-made to your own situation, available whenever or wherever you need it.

How often do you recommend using the recorder?

Whenever you feel like it. I probably average once a year, but many people find it helpful on a frequent basis, sometimes even daily.

Daily? Isn't that a bit excessive?

Not if that's what it takes to do the job. Sid Caesar, who had been one of the most popular entertainers in television for many years, found himself in 1979 at the nadir of his career, ravaged by alcohol and drugs, and by the re-

35

sultant feelings of guilt and insecurity. He knew that his career—indeed, his life itself—depended on kicking those two addictions, but like most addicts he couldn't face the fact that the time to take such a step was *today*. A daily session with a cassette recorder was one of the things that helped him to end his procrastination. Alone for several months in Paris, where he was making a movie, he spent considerable time each day talking to his tape recorder, sorting out his thoughts, lecturing himself on his self-destructive behavior, discussing his inner conflicts. He talked to the recorder in the morning and again in the evening when he got home, and sometimes had a third "conversation" with himself before going to bed.

It worked. He recovered, and as he notes in his book *Where Have I Been?*[7] he continues to use the cassette recorder every day.

Recorded self-dialogue isn't for everyone, but you might find it worth experimenting with.

But to prepare a tape such as you're talking about requires advance planning if it's to be any good, doesn't it?

Absolutely not! In fact, if you prepare for it you lose the spontaneity that makes it so valuable. *Don't* work from an outline, *don't* have notes, *don't* be self-conscious. Nobody is ever going to hear the tape except you, and if you mess it up you can easily erase it. Just sit down in a completely private setting, close your eyes if you like, and start counseling yourself, saying the things that that stern but understanding Dutch uncle would say to you. Don't hold anything back. Lay it all on the line.

This all sounds easy, but for many people nothing could be harder than what you're asking. This kind of candor, "letting it all hang out," might be attained over

a period of time working with a psychiatrist or a psycho-
therapist, but the notion of sitting down and talking to
yourself—with or without a cassette recorder—seems
strange and unnatural. We've been taught that when we
speak there should be somebody on the receiving end. It
takes two to tango. Or to talk.

Balderdash! Why do you need to sequester yourself with
a psychotherapist in order to verbalize your feelings and
intentions? You know what's bothering you—say so! You
know what needs to be done about it—say so! Draw on your
own insights; tell yourself that you can and will take specific
remedial steps.

Please understand, I do not mean to disparage psychiatry
or clinical psychology, or ministerial counseling, or any other
kind of counseling. Those disciplines have much to offer,
provided the counselor is perceptive and compassionate, and
people who are unable to overcome procrastination and take
charge of their lives after trying the techniques discussed
here should by all means seek professional help. A skilled
therapist—and please note that qualifying word—can be of
great help if you are one of the relatively small percentage
who require such assistance.

But psychiatrists and psychologists in recent years have
increasingly come to the view that most people can find the
answers to their own problems with a little encouragement.
One of the important recent developments in counseling has
been the increased use of the non-directive therapy technique
developed by Dr. Carl Rogers, in which the therapist simply
tries to establish the kind of accepting relationship that encourages the client to clarify and express his feelings and to
work out his own solutions to his problems. If one can find
ways of accomplishing that without the therapist, why not?
At least it's worth a try.

So you would say that the place to begin is with a little self-analysis?

No, that's not quite the right word. It isn't your *self* that you want to analyze, but your *behavior*. And remember that the goal isn't analysis, but change.

When people try to analyze themselves they begin to focus on the past, and when they do that they always find many places to put the blame for their shortcomings—parents, siblings, teachers, fate, the company, the boss, the economy, the system. Even if the analysis happens to be correct it isn't very helpful. So instead of asking such questions as "What's wrong with me?" or "What made me the way I am?", it's far more helpful to ask, "In what ways would I like to change my behavior, and how can I?"

This is the approach a skilled counselor will take. In the early days of psychoanalysis the followers of Sigmund Freud probed extensively into the patient's past; most modern psychiatrists and psychologists concern themselves much more with the present. In his book *Reality Therapy*, Dr. William Glasser says,

> Because the patient must gain responsibility right now, we always focus on the present. The past has certainly contributed to what he is now, but we cannot change the past, only the present. Recounting his history in the hope that he will learn from his mistakes rarely proves successful and should be avoided. From past mistakes the patient learns only that he knew better at the time, yet still did not act on his knowledge. It may be interesting to talk about past errors with friends or family, but it is a waste of time to discuss them with the therapist. The present, the right now, is the critical task, not the easy job of recounting his historical irresponsibility and looking for excuses. Why become involved with the irresponsible person he was? We want to become involved with the responsible person we know he can be.[8]

Note that term *responsible person.* The whole issue of procrastination hinges on that phrase. By definition the procrastinator is behaving irresponsibly, postponing something that should not be postponed. The responsible individual, on the other hand, simply goes ahead and does what needs to be done when it should be done. Irresponsible behavior is typical of childhood; responsible behavior is the hallmark of the mature adult. Irresponsible behavior involves looking for people to blame for things that have gone wrong; responsible behavior involves putting the past behind you and asking, "What can I do *right now* to improve my situation, and move toward my goals?" The techniques we've been looking at are merely ways of asking (and answering) that question.

There's one verbalizing technique you haven't mentioned. Instead of talking to yourself on paper or out loud, or talking to a recorder or consulting a counselor, what about talking with friends?

It can be an excellent idea—or it can be a disaster, depending on how you do it.

If, instead of asking your friends for advice, you *tell* them what you're planning to do about your procrastination, you've made a smart move. I call this Going Public.

Announcing that you are going to get a particular job done by a certain time gives you an added incentive to perform. You've put yourself on the spot. We all hate to embarrass ourselves before friends by having to confess that we didn't do something we openly committed ourselves to do. Going Public provides external reinforcement of your good intentions.

Sometimes, instead of just announcing to another person what it is that you intend to do, it may be helpful to have someone monitor your progress by listening to a progress report from you at prearranged times.

Would you give an illustration of this monitoring process?

A good example is given by Richard Nelson Bolles in his classic book *What Color Is Your Parachute?*, which explains techniques for finding or changing jobs. He points out that for many people the job search is a difficult, unpleasant, frustrating task; consequently, procrastination often becomes a crucial factor. When that happens, he says, "Decide whom you know (spouse, roommate, friend, etc.) that you can take into your confidence about this. Tell them what you need to do, the hours it will take, and how much you need *them* to keep you at this task. Then put down in your appointment book a regular weekly date when they will *guarantee* to meet with you, check you out on what you've done already, and be very stern with you if you've done little or nothing since your previous week's meeting. The more a taskmaster this confidant is, the better."[9]

This process of engaging someone to monitor your activities often works. On the other hand, just seeking advice from a friend on how to overcome your procrastination usually doesn't. When you seek advice, what you get most of the time is either sympathy or a preachment, neither of which is very helpful. And too often you wind up bemoaning your plight or rationalizing your procrastination to your friends, instead of really working out a course of action.

There's another pitfall, even more important. When you ask for unnecessary advice, you are sometimes laying the groundwork for failure. If you can shift some of the responsibility for your decisions to someone else, there's less pressure on you to perform, since you have a scapegoat. It's better to say, "If it's to be, it's up to me." Seek advice or help when you really need it, but be aware that it can be a cop-out.

In summary, then, reinforce your intentions when appropriate by Going Public, telling others what you plan to do. If necessary, even ask them to monitor your progress. But don't try to pass the buck by getting someone else to shoulder part of the responsibility for your decisions. Don't sell yourself short—you know your problems, your goals, and your intentions better than anyone else in the world. You know what you must do if you are going to reach your potential, and you have a stake in the process which no one else has. Remember the old saying: "If you're looking for a helping hand, the place you're most likely to find it is at the end of your arm."

This philosophy of self-reliance is sound, no doubt, but what about the possibility of seeking assistance from a higher source? Doesn't prayer deserve a listing in your catalog of anti-procrastination techniques?

Certainly. It would be folly to overlook a practice that has helped billions of people throughout the ages. If what you are procrastinating on is something important, and if you have religious convictions, by all means use prayer as a means of strengthening your resolve. We've spoken of the benefit you can get from making a commitment to a friend. Obviously, if your commitment is to your Maker instead of to the person sitting at the next desk, your sense of obligation will be infinitely stronger.

And even if you don't have a traditional religious faith, you may find that prayer and meditation can be of help. Benjamin Franklin, who had strong reservations about all of the established religions of his time, nevertheless made it a practice to begin each day with the following prayer:

> O powerful Goodness, bountiful Father, merciful Guide: Increase in me that wisdom which discovers my truest interests; strengthen my resolutions to perform what wisdom dictates. Accept my kind offices to thy other children, as the only return in my power for thy continual favors to me.[10]

41

The phrase "strengthen my resolutions to perform what wisdom dictates" is another way of saying, "Help me to avoid procrastination." If Ben Franklin, the epitome of self-reliance, found it worthwhile to seek divine intercession to strengthen his resolutions, perhaps we should all consider it. Like Franklin, most of us need all the help we can get.

Taking the Second Step

You now have quite a few options that can be worked into your antiprocrastination game plan. Let's list them:

1. *Pigeonholing*
2. *The Salami Technique*
3. *The Leading Task*
4. *The Five-Minute Plan*
5. *The Worst First System*
6. *The Balance Sheet*
7. *The Journal*
8. *Self-dialogue*
9. *Tape Talk*
10. *Going Public*
11. *The Monitor Method*
12. *Prayer and Meditation*

So now you have four lists of problems and a dozen suggestions for dealing with them, and you're probably a bit bewildered by all the possibilities. Your inclination may be just to apply as many techniques as you can to as many problems as you can, in which case you are emulating the character in one of Stephen Leacock's stories who flung himself upon his horse and rode madly off in all directions.

Don't make that mistake. Look over your lists and select a single item on which to focus first. Perhaps it would be well to start with something not too ambitious: an overdue letter, an unpleasant phone call, a long-delayed oil change. Whatever you select, put everything else out of your mind for the moment. Take a sheet of paper, and at the top write what it is you have selected. This psychologically seals your decision; now you have a specific problem to focus on and have made a commitment to solve it. It's time to lay out your game plan.

First, use the Pigeonholing Technique we discussed. And do it on paper.

Next ask yourself, in view of the label you have now attached to your problem, what seems to be the best weapon with which to attack it? It should be suited to the magnitude of the problem—if the selected task is getting your oil changed, I doubt that you would choose No. 7, 9, or 12; you don't use an artillery shell to kill a gnat!

Whatever you do, though, don't get sidetracked. Finish the task you've selected before moving on to a second one. Get the good feeling that comes with success, even in some small matter.

Now look over your lists and set additional priorities. Choose one item from each of your four lists and put a star by it. Next set a date for each of the selected ones—if not the date when you are going to complete the task, at least the date on which you are going to tackle it. Today's date, of course, should be by the highest priority item.

And don't wait until you've read the rest of the book— you know what needs to be done, and it's important to get some action under way.

Now!

Step 3

Overcome Fear of Failure

Is there any one emotion that, more than any other, causes procrastination?

Yes. Fear in its various guises is at the bottom of much of our procrastination. It figures especially in our putting off really important things, as distinguished from simply bothersome chores like cutting the grass or washing the car.

Fear of what? What kinds of fear preclude action?

Fear of failure, fear of self-disclosure, fear of ridicule, fear of the unknown, fear of falling short of perfection, fear of confrontation, fear of pain, fear of risk, even fear of success, to name just a few.

45

And the most common of these is—?

Fear of failure. The realization that what you want to do may not work out, and that you will then have to admit to yourself and possibly to others that you didn't succeed. Many people are immobilized by such thoughts.

But that's understandable, isn't it? You can't blame people for being afraid to stick their necks out when there's a chance they may lose them.

True, but one's neck is seldom at stake, although we often act as if it were. Failure doesn't mean annihilation or disgrace or an end of opportunity. It usually means a temporary setback and nothing more. Thinking of it that way can preserve your morale, your optimism, your zest. In short, it can change your life.

As a matter of fact, not only is failure seldom a disaster, but it can actually have a benign aspect. It can serve a useful function, and can be thought of as a plus rather than as a minus.

Hold on, now. Everyone knows it's possible to over-react to failure, and of course a person shouldn't toss in the towel because of a single defeat. But to think of failure in positive terms is asking a little too much. We live in a success-oriented society. We honor winners, not losers. We celebrate victory, not defeat. Vince Lombardi summed it all up when he said, "Winning isn't the main thing—it's the only thing!" Success is what life's all about.

I can go along with that. Success *is* what life is all about—provided the word is properly defined. Success doesn't mean the absence of failures; it means the attainment of ultimate objectives. It means winning the war, not every battle. Lombardi was no stranger to defeat—while he was coach at Green Bay the mighty Packers went down to defeat 39 times.* Babe Ruth struck out 1,330 times, far more than anyone had ever struck out before. But we judge these men on the basis of their achievements and think of their defeats and failures as mere footnotes to their careers.

However, failure is not just a footnote or an irrelevancy; it is often an ingredient in long-term success. Each failure is a lesson, or can be, if we'll let it. In the words of golfer Tom Watson, "You learn how to win by losing." With failure we have a chance to examine our errors, and to analyze what we might do differently next time around.

I still remember the shock I felt when, as a boy, I spilled a can of paint on the living room rug. As he helped me clean it up, my father said, "Nothing is ever a total disaster if you can learn a lesson from it." That little disaster is still paying dividends—I think about it every time I pick up an open paint can, and I'm just a bit more cautious than I otherwise would be.

Once you learn to think of mistakes and failures as potentially useful experiences, you become more willing to risk failure, and fear becomes less inhibiting.

This healthy attitude toward risk and toward failure is one of the hallmarks of what are often called "self-actualizing" people. Gail Sheehy refers to such people as "pathfinders," those whose lives are "complex models for lives truly worth living." Her extensive research indicates that these exceptionally effective people, when faced with risk and uncertainty, turn most often to four coping devices:

Work more.
Depend on friends.
See the humor in the situation.
Pray.

* Including preseason and postseason games.

In contrast, among the "low well-being" people in her study the four most common responses to rough passages were:

Drink more, eat more, take drugs—indulge.
Pretend the problem does not exist.
Develop physical symptoms.
Escape into fantasy.[1]

In light of what we have been discussing, it is significant that *each of these last four responses is a procrastination technique*, a means of avoiding constructive action.

Gail Sheehy found that roughly half of the outstanding people she identified as pathfinders admitted to having "failed at a major personal or professional endeavor," but that almost every one of them had the same response: they found the failure a useful experience and said they were better off because of it. As she points out, "Knowing that one has survived a failure adds to the armor needed during time of risk, transition, and uncertainty ahead."

Okay, let's admit that valuable lessons can be learned from failure and that surviving failure can strengthen the ego. Aside from that there isn't much to be said for it, is there?

Yes, there is one other important benefit connected with failure. In many situations, successes tend to occur in fixed proportions to attempts. The more often you try—and the more failures you chalk up—the more successes you have.

Would you illustrate what you mean by that?

Suppose your job involves calling on customers, selling on commission. From analyzing your records you learn that on the average you make one sale out of every five calls. Of course, anything you can do to increase that ratio is desirable. But aside from that, even *without* improving your technique, you can increase your income simply by increasing the number of calls you make—in other words, by getting more "failures." At your present rate, to make one more sale per week you need make only one more call each day. Each of those extra calls, even though unfruitful, should be thought of as an accomplishment and not a failure because it has moved you one step closer to your next sale.

People who sell on commission usually learn to think that way. Otherwise they soon find themselves in the Slough of Despond, feeling discouraged and rejected. If they fail to close a sale, having made the best presentation they were capable of, they give themselves credit for having done their best, and move briskly to the next prospect. Failures aren't fun, but they go with the territory.

To take another example, consider a baseball player. Even the best hitters can count on a hit only about once out of three times at bat; the other two times they are going to fail in their goal, which is to get on base. But because the odds are 2-to-1 against success do they therefore try to postpone their turn at bat? Of course not. *And yet that is the very attitude that many procrastinators take.* Knowing that failure is probable, or at least possible, they postpone the very effort that could, if successful, cancel out a large number of failures!

It seems almost as if you are recommending a complacent attitude toward failure.

Not at all. Success is always the goal, but don't dread failure to the extent that you lapse into inaction. Realistically appraise the chances for success, and then, if the facts warrant it, act—even though it means risking imperfection or failure. The important thing is to act, not to act flawlessly.

The late psychologist Abraham Maslow once related an incident that illustrates this point. Referring to a talk with an artist whom he described as "a real artist, a real worker, a real achiever," he said,

> He kept on pressing Bertha (my wife) to get to work on her sculpture, and he kept on waving aside all her defenses and her explanations and excuses, all of which were flossy and high-toned. "The only way to be an artist is to work, work, work." He stressed discipline, labor, sweat. One phrase that he repeated again and again was "Make a pile of chips." "Do something with your wood or your stone or your clay and then if it's lousy throw it away. This is better than doing nothing." He said that he would not take on any apprentice in his ceramics work who wasn't willing to work for years at the craft itself, at the details, the materials. His good-by to Bertha was, "Make a pile of chips." He urged her to get to work right after breakfast like a plumber who has to do a day's work and who has a foreman who will fire him if he doesn't turn out a good day's work.[2]

"Make a pile of chips." A good motto to live by.

Sometimes, though, dealing with fear of failure isn't as simple as just forcing yourself to "make chips." Sometimes a vague dread of what might happen causes you to keep putting off the desired action. How do you deal with that?

That term vague dread holds the clue. As long as your fears are vague and undefined they are impossible to deal with, so the first step is to make them specific, concrete, identifiable. Pin down exactly what it is you're afraid of.

This seems to be another application of what you referred to earlier as Pigeonholing.

Exactly. The point is that it's difficult to deal with something that's hazy and general, whether you're talking about fear, procrastination, or any other problem. If you go for a medical checkup and announce that you don't feel well, you aren't given a prescription. Instead, the doctor begins to probe for more specifics. Until a precise label can be attached to your ailment it's pointless even to think about remedies.

But in this case we've already identified the ailment and labeled it: the label is fear. Fear of failure.

You must push beyond that; it's still too general. Exactly *why* do you fear failure in this particular case? As you dig deeper you may realize, for example, that what you really dread is the embarrassment that would result from that failure. You would have to admit to your associates that you bombed, and that's what's really bothering you.

Now you have put your problem into a pigeonhole labeled Embarrassment Before Associates. You still haven't solved your problem, but you have at least isolated it. Now, instead of trying to deal with a generality—fear of failure—you are dealing with a specific—your embarrassment when your associates would become aware of that failure. Now you can ask yourself some pertinent questions, such as:

Would my failure really be such a big deal with my co-workers? Would they really care that much? What difference does it really make how they feel? What specific action might they take as a result of my failure, and how serious would that be? Suppose they ridicule me; I wouldn't like it, but what harm would be done? And in case I am openly criticized for my failure, what would be my best response? What about the other side of the coin? Wouldn't at least some people admire me for sticking my neck out, even if they didn't say so? And if I do fail, what lessons will I have learned? Putting my failure aside for a moment, what are my chances of success? Am I worrying too much about potential embarrassment which isn't all that likely anyway? What about the respect I may earn from those same associates if I succeed? And aside from all that, am I giving too much consideration to the question of what other people will think? What about my own feelings? Win, lose, or draw, am I not likely to respect myself more knowing that I had the guts to stick my neck out and risk embarrassment for a worthwhile objective? How will I feel about myself if I don't have the courage at least to give it a whirl? It's decision time, so am I going to do it or not? What's the first step? What am I waiting for?

Note that these questions won't even be asked unless you first have clarified precisely what it is that you're afraid of. Elementary as this sounds, most people simply don't take the trouble. In business management we see this blunder every day: a problem is presented in a staff meeting, and people immediately begin to suggest solutions—when the discussion would be far more fruitful if they were to forget about solutions for the time being and probe more deeply into what the problem *really* is, as distinguished from what it appears to be.

But suppose all your probing still leaves you uncertain as to how to proceed. You understand the problem, and you understand your fears, but they are still there. You can't wish them away; what do you do?

When you can't diminish your fears simply by analyzing them—and believe me, you can do so more often than you would expect—the next step is to ask yourself how you would proceed if you *weren't* afraid, and then act in precisely that way. This has been called the Turenne Method, named after the great seventeenth-century French marshal-general Henri de Turenne.

What did he do that was so outstanding?

He did the same thing that countless other courageous people have done throughout the ages, but it has become associated with his name. Many times during the Thirty Years' War, Turenne led his army successfully against superior forces, marching boldly into combat at the head of the attacking unit. When someone once praised him for his courage he replied, "Of course, I *conduct* myself like a brave man, but all the time I'm feeling afraid. Naturally, I don't give in to the fear, but say to my body, 'Tremble, old carcass—but walk!' And my body walks."[3]

That's the ultimate answer to fear. Don't try to deny its existence. You can't fool yourself into thinking you're not afraid or anxious, and it's nothing to be ashamed of, anyway. Acknowledge the fear—but then *act as if it didn't exist*!

That sounds fine, but in actual practice it's not all that easy.

Of *course* it's not easy—I didn't say it was! What I said was that it works. People who require an easy solution to every problem might as well resign themselves to a life of disappointment.

The point is that while this technique of "acting as if" is not always easy, nevertheless anyone can use it. And when you do, it not only enables you to get the task done, but it builds your ego. You develop a self-image of boldness, instead of thinking of yourself as a victim of an invincible enemy called fear.

Of course, the technique can be used to develop other traits as well as self-confidence. William James and Friedrich Nietzsche both commented at length on the useful role this process can play in life, actually changing the realities of our existence. Thus, William James noted that whether we believe God exists or not, "We can act *as if* there were a God; feel *as if* we were free; consider Nature *as if* she were full of special designs; lay plans *as if* we were to be immortal; and we find then that these words do make a genuine difference in our moral life."[4]

Hold on a moment. There's one part of that quotation that might easily be misinterpreted, namely the suggestion that we make plans as if we were to be immortal. Isn't that precisely the attitude that sometimes causes procrastination?

Quite so. I suspect that what James meant was that if we knew we had an eternity in which to enjoy the fruits of each day's labors—or to suffer the penalty of slovenly performance—we'd make a special effort to do each day's work well. Dealing with this same theme, journalist Harry Golden said, "The best thing to do is to start out each day with one idea in mind—that you will live forever. And keep going. Start a major alteration on your house at the age of 70, and at 75 enter upon a whole new course of study or learn a new language. Just keep going as though it will never end. And when it does come, you'll hardly notice it."[5]

Sound advice, no doubt, but you're digressing. Let's get back to the fear problem. You contend that the first step in combating fear is to examine it and pinpoint its cause and its nature. Then, if this scrutiny fails to exorcise it, you recommend that one simply act as if it didn't exist. So you're saying, if you lack courage to act, act courageous.

Right. It isn't a new idea. It was Shakespeare's Hamlet, you'll recall, who said, "Assume a virtue, if you have it not."

But it sounds simplistic. If fear could be conquered that easily we surely would have heard more about this marvelous remedy. People would use it every day!

As a matter of fact they do, usually out of desperation. The child who whistles a happy tune despite fear of the dark, the boxer who climbs into the ring with a confident air even though he knows he's up against a stronger opponent, the comedienne who gives the audience a warm friendly smile even though she senses hostility—all of these people are behaving in such a way as to mask their true feelings, and are gaining courage and diminishing their fear thereby.

But there's one important difference between them and the procrastinator. These people are in situations where they are more or less compelled by circumstance to "put on a happy face." Short of settling for humiliation, there's not much else they can do. But that's not true of the procrastinator, who isn't facing the "moment of truth" but is avoiding it by simply postponing action, pretending that the delay is for some good reason.

In other words, most of us use the Turenne Method when we are compelled to. I'm suggesting that we go one step further and use it when we're *not* compelled to, when we're tempted to delay instead. It's too valuable a tool to be used only as a last resort.

There's one thing about this approach that is troublesome. It seems a bit hypocritical. There's emphasis these days on candor, authenticity, "telling it like it is." But you seem to be advocating that by our actions we deny our true feelings and tell it like it isn't.

Not at all. When you are teetering on the brink of procrastination you are being pulled by two opposing forces.

55

One voice within you, based on emotion, is saying, "There's unpleasantness involved, there's work, there's risk—so I won't do it now; I'll put it off until another day." Your better self, based on reason, is saying, "It won't be more pleasant, or easier, or less risky at a future time—in fact, it will be even more difficult, because of the penalties of delay. It makes sense to do it now and get it over with." It's up to you to decide which of these two voices you will listen to. By selecting the voice of reason instead of the voice of fear you aren't betraying your inner self—you're merely giving expression to the honest conviction instead of the irrational impulse. There's nothing hypocritical about that!

You've discussed this approach in connection with overcoming fear. Is it equally useful in dealing with other inhibiting emotions?

Yes. Whether your failure to act is a result of fear, boredom, depression, shyness, fatigue, unwillingness to tolerate discomfort, or just plain laziness, you'll find it useful to *act as if* you possessed the opposite attribute. Before you act, however, you may find it useful to try imaging.

Imaging? What's that?

The term was coined by Norman Vincent Peale, but the procedure, which has received renewed attention in recent years, is centuries-old. It involves picturing yourself in vivid, specific terms, actually doing the thing you want to do, rehearsing it in your mind. Don't just *think* about doing it, but *see* yourself doing it. Get a clear mental image of yourself performing each step. The psychological effect of this imaginary run-through can be dramatic.

Many athletes have used this technique since publication of *The Inner Game of Tennis*[6] and other books on improving athletic performance by mental practice. But leading sports figures have used the technique for a long time. The great

Ben Hogan, for example, always went through a golf shot mentally, including the follow-through, before making it, and then would depend on what he called his "muscle memory" to execute the shot correctly. Research with basketball players has shown that players who practice in their imagination can greatly increase their accuracy in free throws.

Yes, but now you're talking about development of physical skills. Can the technique be transposed effectively to something like overcoming procrastination?

The principle is universal. Once you have done something—even if only in your mind—it's easier the next time. The relatively easy mental performance paves the way for the more difficult actual performance, whether it's making a golf shot or confronting an unpleasant situation. In either case you have established a mental groove to follow. It's a way of easing into a task when some fear or inhibition makes it difficult for you to just up and do it.

Emerson once said, "The greater part of courage is having done it before." And the next best thing to actually having done it before is mentally having done it before.

So what you recommend is that when people find themselves at an impasse, unable to get started on a task, they should first think about doing it, and then—

Hold on a minute—that isn't what I said at all! And when people try this technique and don't get results, it's because they do just that: they *think* about doing the task. They think about the pitfalls and the problems and the possibilities of failure, and the more they think the more the fear builds up. All they are doing is fretting!

No, at this point you don't want to *think* about doing the task; you want to *see* yourself doing it. Instead of analyzing and weighing and speculating, you want to observe mentally, just as if you were watching a videotape of yourself

57

in action. Thinking has its place, but what we're talking about here is mental role-playing. Quite another thing.

Let's suppose, for example, that your boss has gone back on a promise concerning your work assignment and you have been putting off a confrontation on the matter, although you know you owe it to yourself to speak up. Analyze the facts of the situation, of course, but don't let it go at that. Put the analysis behind you and mentally go into the boss's office. Visualize the boss asking you to sit down, inquiring what's on your mind. Hear yourself opening the discussion and explaining your feelings. Now imagine the boss explaining the reasons for reneging, and hear yourself responding to that explanation calmly, confidently, unapologetically. If you are uncertain what tack the confrontation is going to take, try two or three different scenarios, but in each case *observe* yourself making the response you would like to make if you had no qualms—mentally *acting as if* you had the self-assurance you would like to have. Then, having gone through the imaging process, take the next step: carry out your intentions, acting like the confident person you just saw in your mind's eye.

Are there other techniques that can be helpful in coping with fear?

Yes. One is the exact opposite of the one we have been discussing—instead of imagining yourself succeeding at the task, imagine everything going wrong, in the worst possible way.

That doesn't make sense. By using the opposite of the imaging technique, wouldn't you create a negative image, and thus get the opposite effect?

You'd think so, but it doesn't work that way. By exaggerating your fears you make them look ridiculous, and your sense of humor usually restores your perspective. Either that or you will realize that even the worst possible scenario isn't so terrible after all.

Bertrand Russell was an advocate of this ploy. He urged considering "seriously and deliberately" the worst that could happen in any frightening situation. Then, he said, "having looked this possible misfortune in the face, give yourself sound reasons for thinking that after all it would be no such very terrible disaster. Such reasons always exist, since at the worst nothing that happens to oneself has any cosmic importance. When you have looked for some time steadily at the worst possibility and have said to yourself with real conviction, 'Well, after all, that would not matter very much,' you will find that your worry diminishes to a quite extraordinary extent."[7]

Thomas Carlyle, in his grandiloquent style, describes this process:

> I lived in a continual, indefinite, pining fear; tremulous, pusillanimous, apprehensive of I knew not what . . . when, all at once there rose a thought in me, and I asked myself: "What art thou afraid of? Wherefore, like a coward, dost thou forever pip and whimper, and go cowering and trembling? Despicable biped! What is the sum-total of the worst that lies before thee? Death? Well, Death; and say the pangs of Tophet [hell] too and all that the Devil and Man may, will or can do against thee! Hast thou not a heart; canst thou not suffer whatsoever it be; and, as a Child of Freedom, though outcast, trample Tophet itself under thy feet, while it consumes thee? Let it come, then; I will meet it and defy it!"
>
> And as I so thought, there rushed like a stream of fire over my whole soul; and I shook base Fear away from me forever. I was strong, of unknown strength; a spirit, almost a god. Ever from that time, the temper of my misery

was changed: not Fear or whining Sorrow was it, but Indignation and grim fire-eyed Defiance. . . . It is from this hour that I incline to date my spiritual new-birth . . . perhaps I directly thereupon began to be a Man.[8]

Your experience with this technique may not be quite so dramatic as this, but I think you'll find it helpful to ask yourself, as Carlyle did, "What is the sum-total of the worst that lies before thee?"

Better still, use a combination of the techniques we've been discussing. When fear causes you to procrastinate, first imagine yourself succeeding gloriously, then ask yourself what's the worst that could happen—and then ask what's more *likely* to happen. It will be something between the two extremes and will probably be something you can live with.

Would you give an example of what you've just suggested?

Suppose you'd like to learn Spanish. It would be useful to you in your work but not essential, so you've been putting off registering for the class. You analyze the reasons and realize your procrastination stems from fear of failure, fear of competing with younger students who might have more supple minds and perhaps even Spanish-speaking backgrounds.

First, imagine yourself successfully learning the language; picture yourself meeting friendly and interesting people, in the class and beyond, conversing with them in Spanish; envision yourself enhancing your status within the organization you work for because of your new-found skill. See yourself traveling in Spanish-speaking countries with new freedom, new appreciation of the culture.

Now envision the worst. The worst that could happen would be to flunk out of the course. Mentally paint a terrible picture of the instructor ridiculing you, all the other students far outperforming you. So what? You could simply resign and nobody would really care. You wouldn't have lost much except some time. The experience would be distasteful, but you realize that you certainly could handle it.

Now ask yourself what is most *likely* to happen. You probably won't star, but you aren't likely to be ridiculed either. Chances are you'll do at least as well as the average and your shortcomings will hardly be noticed. And although you may have some difficulties gaining proficiency, you realize that you definitely would gain something worthwhile by the experience. Your fear now begins to dissipate and you are more likely to be able to take the plunge.

One more thing to be said about fear: don't just think of it as an enemy to be overcome—think of it also as something that can often be quite useful, a beneficial stimulus. For example, your fear may result from inadequate preparation for some task you are contemplating. In that case, instead of trying to find ways of acting despite the fear you should be looking for ways to make the fear unjustified, by getting the additional information or training you need. The greater the fear, the greater the stimulus can be. Thus, your fears can be made to work for you rather than against you.

Finally, there's an old admonition worth repeating whenever you are tempted to postpone a desired action because of fear or uncertainty:

> Don't worry about what's ahead.
> Just go as far as you can:
> From there you can see farther.

Taking the Third Step

From your four lists, select ten things that you would like to do but are afraid to do, or that have an element of risk. (You needn't limit yourself to those four lists, of course. Perhaps other ideas will occur to you that you hadn't previously considered.) Now assign an arbitrary date to each one—at least one task per day—and make a note on your desk calendar or in your tickler file and resolve that on that date you are going to employ the techniques discussed in the preceding chapter, and get the exhilaration that comes from surmounting fear. Start with the easiest one on the list and work up to the most difficult as your mental muscles get toned up.

When you finish doing the things you selected you're going to feel rather proud of yourself. While you are still savoring the fruits of your achievement, clinch the lesson by a memo to yourself or a journal entry summarizing what you've learned.

Now!

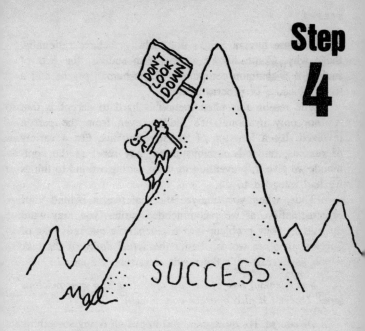

DON'T LOOK DOWN

SUCCESS

Overcome Fear of Success

You list fear of success as one cause of procrastination. That sounds a bit far-fetched. Surely nobody dreads success!

Quite the contrary. Millions do. They have a secret determination to fail, and they are invariably successful— that is, successful in their effort to fail.

But the idea is ridiculous. If you didn't want to reach your goal why would you establish it? Why would anyone attempt to do anything and sabotage his own efforts by trying to fail?

Because human beings don't always behave rationally, that's why. Contradictory as the term sounds, the fear of success is a common component of the human psyche and a frequent cause of procrastination.

The reason this phenomenon is hard to accept is that it's not only irrational, it's hidden, even from the person involved. It's a function of the subconscious. For a variety of reasons, our subconscious mind may rebel at the commands we give it, preventing us from getting around to things we had intended to do.

Thus, when you analyze the real reason behind your procrastination, as we recommended earlier, you may wind up putting your problem into a pigeonhole marked Fear of Success. In other words, it isn't the actual *doing* of the task which you dread—it's the *result* of getting it done.

You speak of fear of success operating at a subconscious level. Doesn't it also operate consciously?

Of course. It's quite common to put off doing something because you have determined that the result of doing it would be contrary to your best interests. In that case it can hardly be called procrastination. You have simply decided that it's not smart to do it, so you abandon the idea. Good thinking—nothing wrong with that.

What causes the serious problems, though, is when you give yourself contradictory signals. Your conscious mind says, "I should do this, and I believe I can," but your subconscious says, "If I succeed in doing it, I'll be sorry." And instead of calmly studying the situation and making a rational decision as to which way to go, you refuse to think about it, leaving it in limbo. In the meantime, because of the stress caused by your irresolution, you are experiencing the tension, the depression, perhaps even the headaches that come from being in a double bind.

This is still a little hard to grasp. Could you give an example of how it works?

Sure. Suppose you are dissatisfied with your income and decide that you'd like to try for a promotion, which would bring an increase in pay. But somehow you never get around to making your move. You don't take the training that's a prerequisite for the promotion. Now, on the surface it might appear that you just haven't gotten around to applying for the training; it has just slipped your mind. What with all the other things you've been doing lately, you just plain forgot, or you've been too busy.

If you dig a little deeper, you might decide that your problem is fear of failure. The job might not materialize, in which case taking that training course would have been a waste of time. And there would be embarrassment because of having failed.

If you continue to dig still deeper, however, you might find that's not the real reason, either. Down at a third level there's something you weren't aware of—a fear of what would happen if you *did* succeed in getting the promotion. You would have new responsibilities, you'd be working in an unfamiliar environment, you'd experience envy from old friends who would resent your promotion, you'd be making tougher decisions, you'd be working longer hours. The subliminal awareness of these imagined difficulties cools your ardor, and you don't make the moves necessary to get the promotion.

And the point is, you don't realize why. If those new responsibilities really *are* too much for you, if you really *can't* stand the heat that goes with that promotion, then it makes sense to stay out of the kitchen. Trouble is, you haven't carefully thought it out and reached that conclusion. Instead, you're kidding yourself into thinking that the problem is either forgetfulness or being "too busy."

Drag your fears out into the open. Label them for what they really are. Then you can look at them from every side and reach a decision based on realities.

And incidentally, any time you put your problem into the Fear of Success pigeonhole, it's time to sit down and have a long, heart-to-heart chat with yourself—or with your therapist.

Why do you say that?

Because you're in a double bind. You're being torn by conflicting pressures. You are unsure of your goals, since the things you've been telling yourself you want aren't what you really want, in view of the price involved. To use a term that's in vogue among psychologists these days, you're not being "authentic" in your dealings with yourself. And procrastination is never the answer—it only makes matters worse.

You mention the "price" involved in having reached a goal. Exactly what do you mean by that?

There are two sides to every coin. No matter how desirable a goal may be, there are some negative consequences of having reached it. Fame means lack of privacy; wealth draws envy; growth fosters higher expectations; a promotion entails more responsibilities; a spectacular achievement raises the question of what you will do for an encore.

We are constantly weighing the pros and cons of possible courses of action, deciding in one instance that the advantages offset the disadvantages, in another that the price is too high. But with procrastination that process is circumvented. Instead of objectively considering the price of achieving a goal and then making a decision, the procrastinator decides by default against resolving the matter either way. The will to fail blocks objective consideration.

This will to fail—is that another name for fear of success?

Yes. And it sometimes is known by other terms. In universities, for example, there is a common phenomenon that educators call the Ph.D. syndrome. A student decides to obtain a doctorate, but somehow, after completing all of the course work and most of the dissertation, never gets around to finishing those last few pages. There are always some more authorities to consult, more finishing touches to add. Success in obtaining the degree would suddenly confer new status and new responsibilities, ending the sheltered life-style of the student. Fearing such change, and the risk it entails, the perpetual student procrastinates in order to delay success (or even to assure failure) in the pursuit of that advanced degree.

Psychologist Abraham Maslow called this phenomenon the Jonah complex.

Why?

The Bible says that Jonah, who apparently was an eloquent preacher, was chosen by God to perform an important mission: he was to go to the city of Nineveh and preach repentance. But Jonah considered this an unpleasant chore, and being a typical procrastinator, decided to postpone the task—perhaps permanently—by running away. Speaking of the reluctance some people have to achieve their potential, Maslow says:

> In my own notes I had at first labelled this defense "the fear of one's own greatness" or "the evasion of one's destiny" or "the running away from one's own talent." . . . It is certainly possible for most of us to be greater than we are in actuality. We all have unused potentialities or not fully developed ones. It is certainly true that many

67

of us evade our constitutionally suggested vocations. . . .
So often we run away from the responsibilities dictated
(or rather suggested) by nature, by fate, even sometimes
by accident, just as Jonah tried—in vain—to run away
from *his* fate.[1]

This tendency also has been called the Icarus complex,
after the mythical Greek youth who achieved his wish to
fly, only to have the heat of the sun melt his wax wings,
plunging him to death.[2] Some people fear that, as in the
case of Icarus, success would bring their ruination; that the
higher they went the farther they would fall.

*But doesn't that myth demonstrate that fear of success
can serve a useful function? After all, if Icarus had been
a little more fearful, he might have kept a closer watch
on his altimeter and avoided disaster!*

No, caution and fear of success are totally different
things. It is prudent, of course, to avoid unnecessary risk
and to set attainable goals (which presumably would not
include such feats as flying near the sun on wax wings).
But having established attainable goals, you should strive
wholeheartedly to attain them. You should not hold back
by procrastination—or any other self-defeating behavior—
in order to hinder your progress toward those objectives
you've decided are worth striving for.

What it all comes down to is dealing with yourself in
a manner that is forthright and logical, instead of devious
and irrational. If for some good reason you've really decided
not to do something, then for heaven's sake don't do it. *But
having made that decision, eliminate the thing from your
mind.* Don't let it remain there in the guise of something
you're "going to get around to one of these days." The accumulation of a bunch of these pseudo-objectives has a debilitating effect; their insistent nagging diverts you from the

matters at hand and prevents you from enjoying your leisure time with a clear conscience.

There's much satisfaction to be had in crossing a difficult item off your "To Do" list once it has been done—but there's almost as much in crossing it off just because you've decided that you definitely don't want to do it after all! The procrastinator doesn't get that satisfaction—he just leaves the task on his mental "To Do" list where it festers indefinitely. So the person who procrastinates because of fear of success puts himself in a no-win situation: he tells himself that he should do certain things, but at the same time at a subconscious level he orders himself *not* to do those things, and through procrastination evades any resolution of the two conflicting commands.

One is reminded of the prayer St. Augustine said he offered as a young man: "Give me chastity and continence, but not just now."

What reasons do people give themselves for not wanting to succeed?

Dr. Martha Friedman, assistant professor of psychiatry at New York Medical College, has made a special study of this phenomenon, and has come up with an interesting collection of answers to that question. She asks students to complete the sentence, "I don't deserve success because . . ."

Some of the typical answers:

Because I lied on my résumé to get the job.
Because it's all been easy for me; it's been tough for my sister.
Because my parents didn't have it.
Because I cost my parents too much money and time.
Because my father made it big; I couldn't compete with him.
Because I am too competitive.

Because I was a bad boy, certainly not as good as my
brother.

Because my mother always wrote my school papers.

Because my husband is not successful.

Because I connived to get where I am; I didn't do it
with dignity.

Because I got it through seduction.

Because I'm lazy.

Because other people deserve it more than I do.

Because I really don't know what the hell I'm doing.

Because I haven't done a bloody thing to help myself.
My father died and left it all to me. I did nothing
to get it. My success came out of tragedy.[3]

These reasons for avoiding success, and for procrastinating on things that would produce success, can generally
be grouped into three categories:

(1) *Faulty logic*. ("My parents didn't have success," or
"It's been easy for me; it's been tough for my sister," etc.) It
doesn't take a genius to recognize that a conclusion that you
don't deserve success for these reasons is simply a non sequitur.
It serves no purpose to stifle your own growth merely because
of what happened or didn't happen to other people. You are
you; they are they. You have a God-given right to use to the
utmost whatever talents you have and you should exercise
that right.

(2) *Past transgressions*. ("I lied," "I connived," "I got
it through seduction," etc.) These past actions may indeed
be reprehensible and they certainly do nothing for your self-
esteem. But to permit guilt for such past events to blight your
future is pointless. Your self-esteem won't be enhanced by
avoiding actions that would help you grow and achieve; on
the contrary, such avoidance merely lowers your self-respect
even further.

A little candor is needed here. Ask yourself what, if anything, can be done to make amends. If some action is indicated, take it. If nothing can be done, put the transgression behind you and let your penance consist of extra efforts to merit honestly any success you may achieve in the future.

And in dealing with guilt, remember the old adage that honest confession is good for the soul. Try discussing your feelings with your minister, priest, or rabbi or with a psychiatrist, psychologist, or other counselor.

Also, don't underestimate the power of a journal to expunge guilt.

(3) *Fear of the responsibilities success would bring.* ("I don't really know what I'm doing," "I'm all hustle, no substance," etc.) Such feelings can, of course, result from one of two things: (a) an honest awareness of your inadequacies and a realization that success would move you to what management specialist Laurence Peter[4] calls your "level of incompetence," where you just wouldn't have what it takes to make the grade; or (b) low self-esteem. If it's the former, the answer is to remedy your weaknesses, if possible, through additional study, work, tutoring, practice, or whatever else may be required. If the weakness cannot be remedied—and let's face it, some cannot—and you realize that you will never be able to handle the success you are halfheartedly seeking, then stop seeking it. Adjust your sights. Set some new goals, more modest, perhaps, but more realistic—things you can really strive for without any holding back. In other words, quit kidding yourself. Stop using procrastination as a substitute for thought. Stop fretting about goals that aren't genuine goals at all.

On the other hand, if low self-esteem is the culprit, as it usually is, the answer is quite different. You must learn to appreciate your strengths, develop a positive self-image, reinforce small successes, be willing to risk, and learn to keep your cool in the face of failure, all of which are discussed elsewhere in this book.

Your tidy little analysis leaves one very big question unanswered: How do you determine which of the two it is? How do you distinguish between genuine inadequacy and low self-esteem?

I wish there were some kind of litmus test that could be used to determine that difference, because it's the central question every person faces in deciding whether to try for any ambitious goal: "Do I have what it takes, or don't I?" No one can answer that question for you. Sometimes you can't answer it for yourself, either, until you've attempted the task and risked the possibility of getting in over your head, making up your mind that you'll give it your best effort anyway.

Let me just say this: chances are, your fear stems from a faulty self-image rather than from incompetence. If you have set a goal for yourself, it is probably something that you could achieve and could handle after achieving it if you would only make your move. Instead we all tend to sell ourselves short, underestimating our abilities. I referred earlier to the belief of distinguished psychologists that most humans use only a small portion of their potential, a belief shared, I think, by all thoughtful observers of the human condition. This means that you have a vast reservoir of unused talent and capability available to you. But if procrastination and timidity keep you from ever opening the floodgates, the reservoir might as well be empty.

Early in this century, the poet Edgar Lee Masters wrote *Spoon River Anthology*, in which the inhabitants of a fictional Midwestern town look back over their lives. If procrastination is preventing you from using your skills to the maximum because of fear of success—or for any other reason— consider the words of Spoon River's Abel Melveny:

I bought every kind of machine that's known—
Grinders, shellers, planters, mowers,
Mills and rakes and plows and threshers—
And all of them stood in the rain and sun,
Getting rusted, warped and battered,
For I had no sheds to store them in,
And no use for most of them.
And toward the last, when I thought it over,
There by my window, growing clearer
About myself, as my pulse slowed down,
And looked at one of the mills I bought—
Which I didn't have the slightest need of,
As things turned out, and I never ran—
A fine machine, once brightly varnished,
And eager to do its work,
Now with its paint washed off—
I saw myself as a good machine
That Life had never used.[5]

Taking the Fourth Step

Comb through your four lists and isolate those items that you've been postponing because you were subconsciously uncomfortable with the implications of success. What would the negative results be in each case if you achieved your objectives? Are they really valid reasons for not wanting to achieve the goal? If so, cross that item off your list, and direct your attention to other matters. If they are not valid, resolve to stop cheating yourself, and establish a timetable for getting them done.

Now!

Step 5

Raise Your Energy Level

You've noted how habits and attitudes and judgments often cause procrastination. But what about a person's energy level? Doesn't fatigue often play an important role in procrastination?

Indeed it does. A person may have a clear idea of what needs to be done and a firm intention of doing it only to find that physical exhaustion causes repeated postponement. Fatigue is one of the most common causes of procrastination.

Fatigue from normal physical exertion is a natural, healthy response, but it tends to be short-lived. Once your body bounces back, you experience an abundance of energy. But chronic fatigue—the kind that gives rise to procrastination—is a malady, and unless it is dealt with, it will thwart your efforts to get things done.

What causes chronic fatigue?

It can have purely medical origins, although it usually doesn't.

Two doctors who have made an extensive study of fatigue, Dr. Leonard Haimes and Dr. Richard Tyson,[1] estimate that only about 20 percent of the people who come to them complaining of persistent fatigue have problems that require actual medical treatment. That 20 percent have a wide variety of problems, such as anemia, emphysema, diabetes, kidney infections, tuberculosis, hepatitis, and chemical or hormonal disturbances resulting from drug use or from natural causes.

What about the remaining 80 percent?

The cause of most fatigue problems is one of three things, or a combination of them. The first one is insufficient exercise.

A regular program of moderate exercise, including aerobic exercise (the kind that increases your pulse rate), will in itself often reduce or eliminate chronic fatigue. But you must do it correctly.

The thing to remember is that the *amount* of exercise you get is not as important as the *frequency*. You can't stay physically fit with a lot of exercise every weekend. You're better off with at least fifteen or twenty minutes of exercise every day or two. And interestingly, researchers have found that there doesn't seem to be much difference between exercising every day and every other day.[2] But when you skip more than one day or limit your exercise to weekends you are cheating yourself. The exercise is not only much less effective but can be dangerous, especially if you are over forty. In an article in the *Journal of the American Medical Association*,[3] Dr. Henry D. McIntosh, a Florida cardiologist, warns that people who exercise only on weekends with no workouts in between are at "great risk" of a heart attack, and the more out of shape they are, the greater the risk.

Look, this is supposed to be a book about procrastination. Aren't you getting off the track?

Not at all. Let's go over it again. One cause of procrastination is chronic fatigue. A major cause of chronic fatigue is lack of physical fitness. And the main reason for lack of physical fitness is insufficient exercise.

I sincerely believe that a regular program of physical exercise can do wonders in cutting down on the tendency to procrastinate. And it's not just the matter of having more physical energy. Exercise also affects your self-image. Being in good physical condition makes you feel more confident, more assertive, more cheerful, so that you are more inclined to tackle the important but unpleasant tasks that you are likely to put off if you see yourself as a self-indulgent slob.

Procrastination isn't an isolated habit. It relates both to physical health and mental outlook. So, to use the word that's in fashion these days, we must take a "holistic" approach.

Okay, so keeping fit to maintain a high energy level is a good thing. Anything else to say on the subject?

Yes indeed. Programmed exercise is only part of the story. There is also the matter of getting the kind of physical activity during the working day that will prevent fatigue.

People with sedentary jobs often get too little activity at their work and consequently become lethargic. We weren't designed to work at a desk or a machine or a computer screen for eight hours at a stretch. These prolonged periods of immobility cause the blood to stagnate in the large muscles.

and in the extremities. The result is a feeling of drowsiness or tiredness, so that when we are faced with an unpleasant, postponable task, the scales are tipped toward postponement rather than toward action.

But many workers have no choice. In an office, for example, most procedures—phoning, paper handling, interviewing, bookkeeping, reading, typing, planning, meeting, researching—are traditionally done while seated. So any "activity" must be accomplished outside working hours, mustn't it?

By no means. In the first place, most of those tasks can be done at least part of the time standing up. Now, of course, if you are an office worker you will sit most of the time, but you should use every opportunity to alternate between sitting and standing to minimize fatigue. For example, you might form the habit of standing when on the telephone. An extra-long telephone cord or a cordless phone can free you from being confined to one spot while phoning.

If you do want to sit, it's often better to sit on the edge of a desk or table rather than sitting plopped in a chair, because you don't remain in the same position for long periods. Hold conferences standing rather than sitting, when possible—they tend to be shorter and more productive that way anyhow.

And a standup work area can reduce fatigue. A counter, a bookcase, a file cabinet, even a makeshift work platform about elbow height—anything that provides an alternative to prolonged sitting—is worth considering.

Of course, standing for long periods can be just as fatiguing as sitting, so if you have a stand-up work station you should have a high stool available. And it should have rungs, or a base on which you can rest one foot while standing, because shifting the weight from one foot to the other reduces fatigue. (The brass rail at the stand-up bar of the old-fashioned saloon was not put there just for decoration!)

A number of business executives in recent years have adopted the idea of a stand-up desk. Among them are the presidents or board chairmen of Prudential Insurance Co., Kellogg Co., Xerox, Koppers Corp., Transamerica Corp., IBM, and G. D. Searle & Co., and the vice chairman of the Federal Reserve Board.[4] But you don't have to work on Mahogany Row to benefit. Anyone who sits a lot should try to devise some kind of stand-up work station.

Is this idea something new?

Hardly. One early user of a stand-up desk was Henry II, king of England from 1154 to 1189, who is said to have been noted for his "enormous energy, executive ability, and administrative skills."[5]

During the Middle Ages the stand-up desk was often used by monks and scholars, and well into the nineteenth century it was common for bookkeepers, law clerks, and others in sedentary occupations to make them less so with a stand-up desk. Among writers who found they could do more and better work while standing are Oliver Wendell Holmes, Ernest Hemingway, Winston Churchill, Vladimir Nabokov, Thomas Wolfe, and Virginia Woolf. A stand-up desk designed by Thomas Jefferson—the one on which he drafted the Declaration of Independence—is now on display at the State Department in Washington, D.C.

Aside from a stand-up desk or work area, any other tips for the sedentary worker?

Yes. Move around as much as possible. For example, go to the other person's office for that conference instead of meeting in yours, if you can. Use the stairs rather than the elevator. Park farther away than necessary to get a bit of extra exercise. Take short walk breaks. Form the habit of a brisk walk after lunch.

And there are simple exercises that can be done in the workplace. Some people keep a few things in their desk to use for exercise—things like a small pair of dumbbells, a tension bar, or various other devices to squeeze, stretch, or pull. Dr. Laurence Morehouse, the noted authority on fitness, claims that the best piece of equipment you can have in an office is an adjustable chinning bar. He recommends that you occasionally just hang suspended from it for a few seconds, letting everything stretch out.[6]

Hold on a minute. That might be okay if you have a private office, but for most people it just isn't practical. Most employers would frown on the use of exercise equipment in the workplace, no matter how much it might reduce fatigue. If equipment is out of the question, what can you do?

Plenty. Although some people prefer to use equipment, it isn't really necessary. Stretching is an excellent activity. So is just tensing various muscles or stressing them against each other (the so-called isometric exercises), many of which can be done even when sitting in a chair while working.

Keep in mind that what we are talking about here is not a physical conditioning program. We are just talking about things you can do to restore circulation of blood stagnating in the extremities and in the large muscles of the body because of prolonged physical inactivity. Better circulation will help the blood do its part to keep you alert and energetic and less prone to postpone tasks until tomorrow.

You mentioned that there are three factors in combating fatigue. Exercise is one. What is the second?

Relaxation.

A desirable thing, no doubt—if one can find time to relax in today's hectic world. What's the third factor?

Hold on—not so fast! Relax! This subject may not seem exciting, but it's more important than you might think, so let's look at it for a moment.

In the first place, just giving lip service to the value of relaxation—which we all do—isn't enough. And it's not enough, either, to plop down in front of the television set for an hour or two every evening with a beer in one hand and a bowl of potato chips in the other. That may be entertainment, it may even be recreation, of sorts—but relaxation it isn't!

Dr. Herbert Benson, a psychiatrist on the staff of Harvard, has made extensive studies on what he calls the "relaxation response," which is involved in transcendental meditation, Zen, yoga, and various other relaxation techniques. He found that these relaxation-producing regimens all have quantifiable physiological effects and that they have four things in common: a quiet environment, a mental device (such as a sound or word or "mantra"), a passive attitude, and a comfortable position to reduce muscular effort to a minimum.[7]

To obtain the relaxation response, sit comfortably, close your eyes, then relax your muscles, beginning with your feet and slowly working up to your head. Breathe through your nose. Say the word *one* as you breathe in, and again when you breathe out. Continue this for twenty minutes. Open your eyes to check on the time, but don't use an alarm. Try this twice a day for several days, preferably not just after eating, and see if it doesn't make you feel calmer, more energetic, more self-assured—and more inclined to tackle some of those unpleasant chores you've been putting off.

What about the role of a nap in combating fatigue?

It can help immeasurably, and it's unfortunate that the siesta hasn't caught on in our culture. Especially for people in middle age and beyond, a brief nap—even fifteen or twenty minutes—in mid-day or mid-afternoon or just before dinner can work wonders in recharging the batteries.

Naps aren't for everyone. Many people simply don't have that option, and there are some who find that instead of perking them up, naps make them feel more lethargic. But many successful people have been inveterate nappers, including such people as Albert Einstein, Thomas Edison, Winston Churchill, Buckminster Fuller, General George C. Marshall, Eleanor Roosevelt, John D. Rockefeller, Margaret Thatcher, and Presidents Truman, Eisenhower, Kennedy, and Johnson. Billy Graham, like many speakers and performers, prepares to address a crowd of 100,000 by taking a nap.

A nap doesn't have to be lengthy; in many cases, just ten or fifteen minutes will suffice.

The fastest napper I've heard of is artist Salvador Dali, who, according to legend, gets by with very little sleep, but takes frequent instant naps. He supposedly combats fatigue by sitting in a chair with his arm hanging down and a spoon resting lightly on his loosely cupped fingers above a tin plate on the floor. Then he closes his eyes and relaxes completely. When he dozes, the spoon drops on the plate and he awakens, refreshed by the sleep he has gained from the time the spoon left his fingers until it hit the plate. (As a young newspaper reporter I once interviewed Dali, and asked him if the story was true. He assured me it was, but the twinkle in his eye left me wondering.)

Dr. Alton Ochsner, the noted surgeon and founder of the famed Ochsner Clinic in New Orleans, told me once that a daily nap was one of the secrets of his seemingly boundless energy. He said he felt that for himself a brief nap in the afternoon was the equivalent of about two hours of sleep at night.

But if you take a nap instead of performing a task, isn't that procrastination?

Not if it restores your energy level and gives you the verve you need to tackle the job more aggressively. But it's true that a nap can be an avoidance device, so you have to decide for yourself whether it will be a help or a hindrance. I urge that you at least experiment and see if you are one of those lucky individuals who can greatly increase their energy levels in the afternoon and evening by a short nap. If you're battling the temptation to procrastinate, there's no use also battling fatigue at the same time, unless circumstances force you to.

You said there were three major factors involved in building a higher energy level. We've discussed exercise and relaxation. What's the third?

Diet. It's a big subject, one we won't go into in depth, but suffice it to say that so far as fatigue is concerned one big culprit is sugar. Most of us eat many times as much sugar as we should.

But isn't sugar supposed to produce energy?

Lots of people think so, but it just isn't true—at least, not in the way they think. Every week the average American eats more than two pounds of refined sugar, much of it hidden as an ingredient in various manufactured foods (one popular brand of ketchup is 29% sugar![8]). If eating refined sugar really produced energy, we would be a nation of live wires and lethargy would be unknown.

It is true that low blood sugar means less energy, but the proper way to maintain the right amount of sugar (glucose) in your blood is through a balanced diet. When you zap your system with *refined* sugar (sucrose) you trigger the release by the pancreas of large amounts of insulin to counteract the sugar shock, and this insulin overcompensates, resulting in a much lower blood-sugar level than you originally had. And one result of this process is fatigue. It sounds complicated, but that's the way it works. (There are other undesired effects of too much sugar, including weight gain and dental caries, but this isn't the place to go into that.)

Look, let's get this straight. You aren't saying that procrastination is a result of eating too much sugar, are you?

Of course not. What I'm saying is that one result of bad dietary practices, such as eating too much sugar, is fatigue. If you are vacillating about whether to go ahead and get a job done or whether to put it off, you will more frequently choose to put it off if you feel pooped. So poor diet doesn't "cause" procrastination, but it may tip the scales. And if bad diet becomes habitual, causing *chronic* fatigue, it can tip those scales dozens of times a day—on matters that don't seem to be related to health in any way whatsoever.

That seems to make sense. Okay, aside from too much sugar, what other aspects of diet are of particular concern in connection with fatigue?

Breakfast is worth special consideration. Starting the day without breakfast—or with just coffee and a sweet roll—is like going into battle without ammunition. And for that mid-morning snack, consider an orange, an apple, a peach, or maybe some celery or carrot sticks instead of that jelly-filled doughnut. Aside from the health benefits, which you're well aware of, you'll get more done as the morning goes on.

What about coffee? It provides stimulation, and therefore increases energy, doesn't it?

Yes and no. The short-term effect of caffeine as a stimulant is well-known, but what many people don't realize is that excessive use of caffeine, whether in the form of coffee, tea, cola beverages, or pills, can *contribute* to fatigue by causing restlessness, tenseness, and irritability, as well as sleep impairment. In fact, Drs. Haimes and Tyson list excessive use of caffeine as one of the most common energy-stealing habits, and recommend cutting down on use of caffeine beverages, or eliminating them completely, as a good way to start a program of increasing energy. (If you're a regular user, they recommend cutting down gradually, to help avoid the headaches that occasionally occur when heavy coffee or tea users abruptly discontinue their intake of caffeine.)

Try to think of energy not as something you *get*—by popping a pill, or drinking a cup of coffee, or eating a candy bar—but as something you *build*, by a sensible diet, including plenty of fresh fruits and vegetables, plus appropriate exercise. Your energy level reflects not so much what you did a half-hour ago as what you've been doing for the past six months.

You said excessive use of caffeine is considered by Drs. Haimes and Tyson to be one of the most common energy thieves. What other habits do they object to?

Smoking, for one. Nicotine is a vasoconstrictor, causing the blood vessels to narrow, which means less blood to the brain. And the blood that does get there contains less oxygen and more carbon monoxide. So the effect is another drain on energy.

This is beginning to read like a temperance tract. You've managed to link low energy levels to sugar, tea, coffee, tobacco; what's next—alcohol?

I'm afraid so. There can be no question that intemperate use of alcohol is a serious energy thief. The person who postpones facing up to a troublesome problem by having a drink instead is so common as to be a stereotype. Procrastination and excessive drinking link up to form a vicious circle: you don't want to tackle that yard work because you feel tired, so you have a drink instead. The drink further weakens your resolve instead of strengthening it, so the job seems more formidable than ever. And when faced with such a formidable job, the only answer is another drink.

Aren't you exaggerating a bit? Many two-fisted drinkers get their unpleasant jobs done despite a predilection for the grape, and as a matter of fact, many doctors believe a drink before dinner may have a therapeutic effect for many people, helping them to relax. And relaxation is helpful in restoring energy levels and maintaining perspective, isn't it?

Look, we aren't talking about a drink before dinner. We are talking about drinking as an alternative to doing.

It would be foolish, of course, to imply a simple cause-and-effect relationship between alcohol and procrastination. But whenever a person chooses to have a drink instead of performing a task that should be performed at that particular time, that person has a combination procrastination problem and drinking problem. And the situation is likely to get worse, because the two tendencies reinforce each other.

So what would you recommend in such cases?

If you must have that drink, I would suggest at least making it contingent on completing the task—not having it before the task, during the task, or (above all) instead of the task.

That pretty well runs the gamut of major vices. About the only one you haven't linked to procrastination is pot smoking.

I'm glad you mentioned that. As a matter of fact, marijuana is another substance that promotes procrastination.

Now wait a minute. Marijuana has been blamed for a lot of things, but isn't linking it to procrastination a bit much?

Not at all. The only reason this aspect of pot isn't mentioned more often, I suspect, is that it's much harder to measure procrastination than it is to measure cell damage, testosterone levels, memory loss, immune system impairment, and respiratory ailments.

But consider one undisputed fact: even people who condone occasional use of marijuana admit that its use by children and teenagers lowers academic performance. And a major reason for that decline in grades, obviously, is that the students become apathetic and procrastinate on homework and on studying.

Dr. Harold Voth of the Menninger Foundation's School of Psychiatry, and chief of staff of the Topeka VA Medical Center, has studied the psychopathology of marijuana use for eight years. Among the characteristics he lists as being related to the pot personality are diminished willpower, the amotivational—or dropout—syndrome, lessened concentration, shortened attention span, diminished ability to deal with abstract or complex problems, emotional flatness, impaired judgment, and lowered tolerance for frustration.[9] Every one of those factors quite obviously is associated with procrastination.

So if you happen to use pot, and if you also find that you just can't get started on projects you consider worth doing, perhaps you should find some more salubrious way of getting your kicks. Think of that marijuana joint as a tiny package of highly concentrated laziness.

All right, granted that such drugs as marijuana and alcohol may promote procrastination, isn't it possible that some other drugs might have the opposite effect? Aren't there some prescription drugs, for example, that might be useful in helping to cope with procrastination?

It's an indication of the malaise afflicting our civilization that so many people are looking for a quick fix—a pill that will replace effort and self-discipline. Such a pill hasn't been produced and never will be.

However, in those cases where fatigue or stress have medical origins, yes, there are prescription drugs that can be helpful. And there's one over-the-counter drug that we don't usually think of in connection with fatigue, but that can be helpful in some cases. As Professor S. Howard Bartley, a noted authority on fatigue, points out,

> A common drug helpful in the alleviation of fatigue is aspirin, which is genuinely effective in dispelling a substantial range of general bodily discomforts. Much indisposition among people at any age stems from relatively minor, but general, aches and pains; and aspirin tends to relieve this common aspect of fatigue. While it might be supposed that aspirin's analgesic (pain-relieving) power might also dull one's sensory activity, alertness tends to be enhanced rather than impaired.[10]

Are there any other things that should be considered in connection with fatigue?

One that should be mentioned is posture. A moderately erect carriage can improve both your energy level and your attitude. It's hard to be a "do-it-now!" person when your shoulders are slumped, your eyes are on the floor, your chin is dragging, and your breathing is shallow and cramped.

But this is so elementary! Most people learned this stuff in the third grade.

True. And forgot it in the fourth. Take a look around any large office, and notice the difference in carriage, in stride, in bearing, between the doers and the duds. Too many people are unaware of their posture and of the effect it has on them physically and psychologically.

Speaking of psychological factors, isn't it true that attitudes and emotions sometimes can be even more significant than the physical causes of fatigue you've been discussing?

Yes. You can make yourself tired just by dreading some frustrating or tedious task. This happens especially when you habitually turn your thoughts inward—when you are preoccupied with how you will feel while doing the task, and with your aches and pains and discomforts—instead of focusing your attention on the task itself.

This pseudo-fatigue cannot be cured by mollycoddling yourself and postponing the job: it is cured by action. Getting involved in the job often takes your mind off your "fatigue," and your energy problem solves itself.

We all know that external events often will cause fatigue suddenly to vanish. Perhaps you are tired, looking forward to a quiet evening at home, when the phone rings and you learn that some unexpected guests are on their way to visit you. As you scurry to tidy up and get yourself presentable the tiredness is forgotten.

The fact that fatigue can be banished instantly by such emotions as excitement, curiosity, fear, anger, and anticipation demonstrates that to a considerable degree it is an ephemeral, controllable condition. It fluctuates not just according to how much we have used our muscles, or according to the time of day or night, but according to our attitudes, our thoughts, our interests. And this means that we can override it—temporarily, at least—by a pure act of will.

You don't mean to say that you can just "think" yourself an extra supply of energy, do you?

I wouldn't put it quite that flatly, but it almost comes down to that. Usually, though, it doesn't result from just gritting your teeth and saying, "I refuse to feel tired." It's more likely to work if you say to yourself, "Yes, I am tired; nevertheless, I am going to force myself to finish this task now instead of putting it off. It may be an ordeal, but the benefits of early completion outweigh the dubious benefits of an unearned rest, so let's have at it." Then, as you become immersed in the work, and in the challenge of completing it before stopping, you find you have reserves of energy of which you were not aware.

You're saying, then, that if you stick with a task despite fatigue you eventually achieve something comparable to the "second wind" that a runner experiences?

Exactly. In fact, William James once used that analogy. He said,

> If an unusual necessity forces us onward, a surprising thing occurs. The fatigue gets worse up to a certain point, when, gradually or suddenly, it passes away and we are fresher than before! We have evidently tapped a new level of energy. There may be layer after layer of this experience, a third and fourth "wind." We find amounts of ease and power that we never dreamed ourselves to own, sources of strength habitually not taxed, because habitually we never push through the obstruction of fatigue.[11]

So don't give in too easily when fatigue seems to block your performance of a task. Analyze the fatigue, as suggested in this chapter, but then, if nothing else works, simply try sticking with the task until you get your second wind.

And if fatigue is really your problem, it might be well to keep in mind another observation made by William James: "Nothing is so fatiguing as the eternal hanging on of an uncompleted task."

Taking the Fifth Step

If you are one of the countless millions of people whose procrastination problems are caused—or intensified—by chronic fatigue, then doing something about this infirmity should be your top priority project.

Don't arbitrarily rule out medical reasons—that's a job for a physician. How long since your last checkup? Have you discussed your chronic fatigue with your doctor? Remember, it may be symptomatic of a number of ailments, so be sure to mention it. And if you're overdue for a checkup, can you think of a better time than this moment to make an appointment?

Once you've eliminated the possibility of conditions requiring medical treatment, you've placed yourself in the much larger group of people whose fatigue problems are their own fault, a result of some type of self-indulgence. Since what's at stake here is much more than just the procrastination habit—it's your health, your energy, your longevity, your zest for living, that we're talking about— resolve to begin immediately to do those commonsense things you know very well you should do, as discussed in the preceding chapter.

Before reading further, while you're in the mood, seal your good intentions by writing down what steps you intend to take. Then celebrate your decision by taking a good brisk walk, or by getting some other appropriate exercise, signaling the beginning of a new routine.

Now!

Step 6

Get Tough with Yourself

All of the advice you're giving out presupposes that the person involved has enough willpower to carry out your suggestions. But, unfortunately, willpower is often in short supply—especially for the typical procrastinator. How can one cope with a lack of willpower?

You have to learn to be tough with yourself.

That's easily said, but it isn't really very helpful. A person who knows how to be "tough" with himself probably doesn't lack willpower, and doesn't procrastinate. What's the answer for the millions who don't have whatever it takes to exercise self-discipline?

There's no such person. We all have the option of using self-discipline if we choose to. We are born with a resiliency, a toughness that can enable us to withstand privation, pain, discomfort, and all the other "natural shocks that flesh is heir to," but in our modern world we have become so accustomed to the easy life that this inner strength is seldom exercised on a day-to-day basis. However, it's still there, dormant, awaiting the circumstances that will call it forth. And when that happens—when some crisis requires a seemingly superhuman display of pluck—we often amaze both ourselves and others with our ability to prevail over adversity.

This may be an attribute of the exceptional individual, but does the ordinary person have this unutilized power you speak of?

Absolutely. It doesn't always come into play, but it's there. This is what leadership is all about. The great leader is the one who has learned how to call forth extraordinary effort from supposedly ordinary people. And, the successful person, the real achiever, is often just an ordinary person who has learned to put forth that extraordinary effort without the urging of someone else. In other words, it isn't that he *has* more inner power—it's that he has chosen to *use* more of what he has.

So there's hope for everybody? No exceptions?

No exceptions. Some may find it more difficult than others to establish and maintain self-control—the person who uses drugs, for example, has a hard row to hoe—but everyone can make progress and can develop a stronger, more reliable will.

How?

By practice. Just as you learn to walk by walking, or to juggle by juggling, you learn to exercise self-discipline by exercising self-discipline. But you don't just "will" yourself the ability to walk or to juggle—you take it one small, tentative step at a time, repeat those small steps until they become habitual, and then take larger steps. Similarly, you can practice exercising willpower in small matters. As your efforts become more frequent and more successful you will naturally try for more challenging victories, until eventually you will reach the point where you can get tough with yourself whenever the situation calls for it. Then, and only then, can you honestly say, as did William Ernest Henley, "I am the master of my fate; I am the captain of my soul."

Then you recommend doing difficult things not just for the intrinsic benefit involved, but because they provide practice in self-discipline?

Correct. Each time you perform a difficult act—or resist a temptation—you make it easier to do so in the future. In the words of Hamlet,

> Refrain tonight,
> And that shall lend a kind of easiness
> To the next abstinence; the next more easy;
> For use almost can change the stamp of nature . . .

So you would compare willpower to a muscle, which grows either stronger or weaker, depending upon whether or not it's used?

Yes. The human mind, like the human body, has an incredible ability to adjust to the demands made on it, and when the demands are steady, regular, and consistent, the result is growth, power, and greater ease of performance. In exercising your will you establish a mental "groove"—a habit pattern—that is deepened with each repetition, but which will gradually fade with lack of use.

Most of us recognize the validity of this principle where physical exercise is concerned. As one leading authority points out, "Exercise benefits do not persist more than a month following cessation of training. The beneficial effects of exercise, like those of food, cannot be stored but must be renewed almost daily."[1] (This explains why so many former college athletes enter middle age with no health advantage over their less athletic peers.)

So it is with self-discipline: it doesn't take long for the psyche to get "out of shape." Nature's law for willpower, as for muscle power, can be expressed in just five words: Use it or lose it.

Do psychologists, then, recommend "flexing" the will regularly?

Indeed they do. One who emphasized this concept many years ago was William James, who put it this way:

> Keep alive in yourself the faculty of making efforts by means of little useless exercises every day; that is to say, be systematically heroic every day in little unnecessary things; do something every other day for the sole and simple reason that it is difficult and you would prefer not to do it, so that when the cruel hour of danger strikes, you will not be unnerved or unprepared. A self-discipline of this kind is similar to the insurance that one pays on one's house and on one's possessions. To pay the premium is not pleasant and possibly may never serve us, but should it happen that our house were burnt, the payment will save us from ruin.[2]

More recently, other psychologists, such as Roberto Assagioli[3] and Boyd Barrett,[4] have urged this approach— the daily performance of seemingly useless acts for the sole purpose of strengthening the will. "Gymnastics of the will," they have been called.

But it seems a shame to select something that is "use-less" when there are so many useful tasks to be done!

True. And I am inclined to disagree with Messrs. James, Assagioli, and Barrett on this point. Instead of performing some useless act just for the sake of exercising the will, I think it makes more sense to select a useful task one has been putting off, so as to get some benefit from the exercise beyond the mere training of the will.

What kinds of tasks do you recommend?

Such things as cleaning your paint brushes or fixing the screen door or cataloging your phonograph records or flushing the sediment out of your hot water tank or weeding through your recipe file. The point is, you don't want to select a task that *must* be done. If you're acting out of desperation you don't get the psychological lift that comes from doing something on your own volition *before* it forces itself to the top of your To Do list. And don't select something that you secretly enjoy doing either. Make this a legitimate exercise in willpower, sticking with an unpleasant job until it's finished. While doing it, think of yourself as being in total control, iron willed, resolute, unyielding—a momentary monomaniac, oblivious to distraction or temptation.

Then, when the task is finished, give yourself a mental pat on the back for your toughness. You've proved something to yourself. Tell yourself that your moral fiber is just a little stronger than it was before you undertook the task. It really is, you know.

And remember that the task you select should not be a major one—those will come later, after you've acquired some calluses on your psyche. Don't try to revolutionize your behavior overnight. Shape it gradually, just as you would build your biceps gradually. And keep in mind that a one-time experience won't have much effect, so repeat it frequently.

Many of the tasks you will select for this exercise no doubt will be drawn from your lists of things you are procrastinating on. In fact, if you do this every day, you may be surprised one day to find that you've exhausted your lists!

The first step, though, is to decide which tasks you will use as exercises—and this brings us to another area where you have to learn to be tough with yourself.

What's that?

Decision making. Fortitude in getting a task done is one thing, but it's equally important to be tough with yourself in deciding which task to do, forcing yourself to choose promptly instead of endlessly vacillating among various possibilities.

Indecision is, of course, simply one way of procrastinating, and like all forms of procrastination it drains energy, causes stress, creates an emotional barrier, lowers self-esteem, and prevents things from getting done. But it is only a habit—which means that it can be changed.

But aren't hasty decisions often unwise? Doesn't a prudent person carefully weigh the pros and cons, consider all the various options, and perhaps even "sleep on it" before making a decision?

In the case of a major decision, that's a good idea. But in the case of the typical day-to-day, garden variety decisions, it's important to do that weighing quickly, make a decision, and then proceed to carry it out and get on with something else, rather than deliberating too long.

Many years ago Napoleon Hill, who had spent twenty years studying the work habits and attitudes of successful and unsuccessful people, put the case emphatically: "Analysis of several hundred people who had accumulated fortunes well beyond the million-dollar mark disclosed the fact that every one of them had the habit of reaching decisions promptly, and of changing these decisions slowly, if and when they were changed," he said. "People who fail to accumulate money, without exception, have the habit of reaching decisions very slowly, if at all, and of changing these decisions quickly and often."[5]

Not everyone agrees completely with that observation. For example, Peter Drucker, the noted management consultant, says, "Among the effective executives I have had occasion to observe there have been people who make decisions fast, and people who make them rather slowly."[6] But making a decision slowly—painstaking evaluation of data—is not the same thing as being indecisive, which involves timidity and irresolution even after the essential data are in.

I would suggest that if you have an important decision to make, one that will profoundly affect you and other people, by all means take whatever time is needed. Rumination and procrastination are two different things. On the other hand, in making the everyday decisions—whether to have the party this weekend or next, whether to serve roast beef or steak, whether to have a large group or small—consider the relevant facts, then force yourself to make a decision and proceed promptly to carry it out.

Decisiveness. There's no habit quite so valuable in helping you to achieve your goals. Demand it of yourself. Insist on it. Then you'll find that instead of sleeping on your problems, you'll be sleeping on your accomplishments.

You'll rest easier.

This philosophy of getting tough with yourself, and making yourself do things you'd rather not, smacks of stoicism, of self-abnegation. Its somehow out of step with the spirit of the times.

It's meant to be. I'm not at all convinced that modern society is marching to the beat of the proper drummer.

We live in a culture that worships comfort. During this century we have seen the greatest assault on discomfort in the history of the human race. We have learned to control our environment with central heating and air conditioning, we have reduced drudgery with machines and computers, we have learned to control pain and depression and stress with drugs and therapeutic techniques, we even provide electronic antidotes to boredom with television sets and videogames.

Most of this is to the good. But unfortunately it has created an impression that the purpose of life is to attain a blissful state of nirvana, a total absence of struggle or strain. The emphasis is on consuming, not producing; on short-term hedonism rather than long-term satisfaction. We seek immediate gratification of our desires, with no penalties.

Life doesn't work that way—at least, not for many, and not for long. One of Benjamin Franklin's favorite sayings was "There's no gain without pain," and it's as true today as when it appeared in *Poor Richard's Almanac.* The great goal of becoming what one is capable of becoming can be achieved only by those willing to pay the price, and the price always involves sacrifice, discomfort, unpleasantness, and, yes, even pain.

Another ingredient in the price is, of course, work. George Bernard Shaw summed up the essence of this subject nicely, I think, when he said, "When I was a young man I observed that nine out of ten things I did were failures. I didn't want to be a failure, so I did ten times more work."

What you say is probably true, but you'll have to admit it all sounds a bit old-fashioned.

Well, I'm not so sure that old-fashioned is a pejorative term.

It's true that our grandparents sometimes carried self-denial and self-restraint too far, and it's easy to find examples we could identify as extreme. But reactions to excess are often excessive, and it's unfortunate that the so-called "culture of narcissism" has completely replaced, for many people, the robust self-mastery proclaimed by Rudyard Kipling:

If you can force your heart and nerve and sinew
    To serve your turn long after they are gone,
And so hold on when there is nothing in you
    Except the Will which says to them: "Hold on"; . . .

If you can fill the unforgiving minute
    With sixty seconds' worth of distance run—
Yours is the Earth and everything that's in it,
And—which is more—you'll be a Man, my son![7]

Today we consider Kipling's writings about an empire with dominion over palm and pine to be relics of a bygone age, which indeed they are. But his veneration of the Will—with a capital W, mind you—is right on, man. Right on.

Taking the Sixth Step

And now, the Moment of Truth. We're going to test your mettle, and at the same time give you a chance to strengthen it and raise your self-esteem a notch. We're going to find out whether you're man or mouse, woman or weakling.

You have those four lists we've been working with. You've crossed off a few things already, but there are a lot left. Take a moment to update each list. Think hard—are there any tasks that should be added? Add them.

Now spread all four lists in front of you. Out of the whole schmear, which is the most unpleasant task? I don't mean the most important, nor the most urgent, nor the one you'd prefer to do. I mean the one you'd most prefer not to do.

Put a big star alongside it.

Now take a deep breath, put the book aside, and . . . do it!

(Yes, I mean now!)

Step 7

Establish an Action Environment

To what extent does the physical environment affect procrastination?

In many cases, it plays a key role; in others it's a minor factor. But it will always encourage or discourage action to some degree, so it must be considered.

What environmental factors are most important in preventing procrastination?

Two of the most important considerations are (1) to have the necessary tools and materials at hand, and (2) to have them organized.

Isn't that first point a truism? Obviously, one cannot do anything without the necessary tools. Why even mention anything so elementary?

Because lack of the proper tools or materials is a very common reason for procrastination. As Sherlock Holmes remarked one time (I think), "The first rule, Watson, is never to overlook the obvious."

Sometimes procrastination resulting from lack of wherewithal operates at the subconscious level. Perhaps you have a desk you want to refinish, but you are bothered by a vague feeling that you don't have everything you need, so you keep putting it off. If you were to make a list of the needed materials you would quickly realize that what's missing is sufficient sandpaper. But you don't take the trouble to make that list, so you fail to pinpoint the problem, and keep procrastinating because of a vague uneasiness about the project. In other words, a mental block.

Or the problem may be at a conscious level. You know you need sandpaper, but you haven't done anything to get it. You tell yourself there's no use starting the project without it, and you're quite right, even though you are doing nothing to act on that realization.

So the first step is to identify what will be needed to do the job—make a list, if necessary—and *focus your attention first upon gathering the necessary tools and materials, rather than on the task itself.* It's surprising, when you analyze why people procrastinate, how often this one simple step would get them off dead center.

You also mentioned having things organized. Exactly what did you mean by that?

I mean that it's important to avoid clutter in the workplace.

A neat, orderly workbench, with each tool hanging in its allotted space, is an invitation to get busy, whereas a jumbled aggregation of wrenches, pipes, hammers, clamps, wire, files, pliers, sandpaper, and half-finished projects stifles enthusiasm and encourages delay and diversion.

The same is true in an office. A tidy desk encourages concentration; a disheveled one is a psychological roadblock.

But that's not always true, is it? Some people accomplish a great deal despite very cluttered desks.

Let's clarify what we mean by a cluttered desk. We don't mean one that just has a lot of papers spread out. If a desk is covered with papers which concern the matter at hand, those are working papers, not clutter. Usually you find that the effective person with a seemingly cluttered desk is merely spreading out working papers. Nothing wrong with that.

But *unrelated* papers are another matter. They vie with each other for attention, obstructing an orderly, concentrated attack on any one problem. To overcome procrastination, you must resist the tendency to devote time or thought to diversionary matters, and that's hard to do when miscellaneous letters, reports, regulations, memos, and magazines are spread out all over the place, catching your eye every few minutes and beckoning you down the Primrose Path. Out of sight, out of mind, as the old saying goes: to avoid distraction, put those extraneous papers where you won't see them.

Now, I must admit that there are some notable exceptions. Not everyone with an untidy desk is ineffective. Some gifted souls are able to rise above environmental chaos and focus on their priorities, but they are rare. For the procrastination-prone person (and that includes you, doesn't it?), a cluttered environment leads to disorganized thinking, which in turn leads to putting things off.

But clutter isn't all that easy to control. Stuff accumulates. Any suggestions on how to avoid it?

If you work in an office, a good place to start is to make it a habit to clean off your desk every evening before leaving work. And I don't mean just to put your paper work in neat stacks, or to store a bunch of things in the IN box. I mean when you leave the office there should not be a single piece of paper on your desk.*

Of course, I don't advocate just shoveling everything into a drawer, either, although that's better than leaving it out. Take a few minutes to go through everything and get it not only off your desk, but where it belongs—in the OUT box, in the To Be Filed box, in the wastebasket, in the To Be Done Today folder (which you will tackle in the morning), or in the To Read stack (which, incidentally, should be on a side table or in a drawer, where it won't be a visual distraction).

If you form this habit you will nip a lot of procrastination in the bud, because papers will no longer float on your desk for days at a time. In addition, you accomplish a number of other things: (1) you will discard more junk, and you will discard it sooner; (2) you will be forced to organize better; (3) you will be less likely to lose papers that otherwise would be mixed in with other paperwork; (4) you will reinforce your resolve to handle each piece of paper only once, which is a basic principle of effective time management, and (5) you will get a psychological lift next morning when you sit down to a clean desk instead of to a depressing accumulation of the preceding day's residue.

Throughout the day, as you handle paperwork, keep in mind the three D's: Do it, Delegate it, or Ditch it. Try

---

* As someone has observed, if you leave two pieces of paper on a desk at the end of the day, in the morning there will be four. The little rascals breed overnight!

to avoid setting things aside to be handled later. Occasionally you must, of course. There is a fine line sometimes between legitimate and illegitimate delay, but use the three D's as your guideline as much as possible.*

Of course, what applies to the office also applies to the shop, the laboratory, the studio, the classroom, or the kitchen. Leave as few loose ends as possible from one day to the next. Every little task left overnight is fertile ground in which the seeds of procrastination can take root.

Another habit to beware of is the practice of putting things away temporarily instead of finally. Why set the wrench on the workbench instead of hanging it on its hook? Why handle anything twice when you could handle it only once?

Filing may be in this category. A few paragraphs back I mentioned a To Be Filed box. This is useful if there is a great deal of filing, or if someone else takes care of it. But if you maintain your own files, and have only an occasional item, it's better to file as you go, because each paper you add to that "file pile" will have to be handled again— a violation of the Do It Now principle, reinforcing a bad habit you want to extinguish.

The Three D's approach sounds logical, but how do you handle the exceptions? There are some things that can't be "Done, Delegated, or Ditched" right now, and which probably shouldn't go into the "To Be Done Today" folder, either, because they are very low priority and perhaps should be handled only if and when there's a slack period. Should there be a special place for these items?

Yes. It is quite true that you should not downgrade your "To Be Done Today" category by including odds and

* For further discussion of effective paperwork techniques, see the author's *Getting Things Done: The ABC's of Time Management* (New York: Charles Scribner's Sons, 1976, 1983).

ends that you know *won't* be done today, and it makes sense to set aside a separate tray or drawer for them. I call mine the Back Burner. (One executive I know calls it the Procrastination Drawer. I don't care for that designation myself, because putting something aside while higher priority items are taken care of isn't quite the same thing as procrastination.) Another executive calls it his Friday Afternoon file. Whatever you call it, if you limit it to very low-priority items, you will find it useful. Some people tell me they find at least half of the things they put in such a category seem to take care of themselves if left alone. But remember, you must set aside some time each week to go through the stack and eliminate the deadwood and handle the rest. Bunching up these low-priority tasks for Friday afternoon seems to work very well for many people.

Each week, as you go through the stack, be on the watch for procrastination, as distinguished from justifiable delay. And beware of leaving things there too long: after something has been in the stack several weeks, face up to the fact that nothing is happening to it, and that nothing ever will unless you rescue it from limbo. Then either set a time to do it, or throw it away. Don't let that file become a depository for tasks that are never going to be done.

In other words, it should really be a back burner—not a graveyard!

You mentioned having a stack of things to read. Are periodicals and other reading material another exception to the Three D's approach?

Definitely. You don't want to "Do" the reading until you have a slack period, you usually can't "Delegate" it, and you don't want to "Ditch" it if it's something worth reading. So make a separate stack—away from your work area—of things you intend to read at leisure. But don't let it become a collection of junk; anything that obviously is not worth reading should be discarded immediately.

And don't overlook the possibility of heading off some of this reading material before it gets to your desk. Try to get your name taken off mailing lists for publications that don't really help you. If possible, have most publications routed to a central point, such as a coffee table in the reception area of your office, instead of having them circulated to each individual in the organization. Do all you can to cut down the amount of nonessential reading matter that flows across your desk.

You seem to feel rather strongly about this. Does reading really contribute that much to the procrastination problem?

For many people it does. Some people—and I'm one of them—find it very difficult to concentrate on a task when there is a seductive publication nearby, beckoning them to peruse its pages. (And when I use the word "seductive" I'm not thinking in the *Playboy* sense—my problem is usually an interesting article in this morning's *Wall Street Journal*.)

Distraction is almost synonymous with procrastination, and all of us procrastination-prone people who like to read are sitting ducks for the wiles and machinations of designing journalists. I've learned that the only way I can avoid the lure of the well-written word is to place tempting publications out of reach and out of sight, to be picked up only on the way to lunch or when I've earned a respite by completing some onerous chore.

Where should reading be done?

Any place except your desk.

We're speaking here, of course, of generalized reading, such as books, newspapers, magazines, and trade or professional journals, as distinguished from reading that is related to a particular task. Try to use your desk for work, and for nothing else. When you want to read the newspaper or browse through a magazine move to another location if you can.

This serves two purposes: (1) It preserves the atmosphere of the desk as a place to *work*, not just a place to *be*, so that whenever you are there your mind tends to be in gear, not in neutral; and (2) the act of moving away from your desk focuses your attention on the fact that you are taking time from productive activity, so that you're less likely to let it get out of hand.

Wait a minute. You don't mean to imply that time spent reading professional publications is wasted, do you? Are you trying to make people feel guilty about doing background reading connected with their business during working hours?

Not at all. It's just a matter of keeping in mind that although such reading may be useful it's in quite a different category from task-oriented reading, and it often gets out of hand. It tends to become excessive, it tends to be done at inopportune times, and it tends to become a diversionary ploy, keeping you from promptly dispatching matters that have greater immediate benefit.

For example, if an attorney is getting bored after several hours of research on a case and decides that a half-hour spent browsing through the latest issue of *Harvard Law Review* would be a welcome change of pace, that may be a good use of time; but by moving to another chair in the office to do the reading, he is making himself aware of the fact that for the moment he's not working for any client. This time is not "billable"—directly chargeable to a specific account—so he tends to keep it to a minimum. But if he stays at his desk and just lets his attention wander to the publication, he's less aware of what's happening and is likely to read longer than he should at this particular time.

Furthermore, when faced with taking an overt action, such as moving from his desk to his guest chair, he may reconsider and decide that this is *not* the logical time for a time-out.

Does this apply to things other than reading? For example, do you recommend getting away from the desk or work station for coffee breaks and lunch breaks?

Definitely. You relax better when away from the work area, and you feel more like working when you return. Unless you clearly distinguish between working and resting you tend to spend much more of your time doing something halfway between—in other words, dawdling.

But what about people who don't feel the need of a break but want a cup of coffee. Do you object to having coffee at the desk while working?

No. Many people seldom take a break, as such, but drink coffee as they work, and I see nothing wrong with that. (They may wind up drinking more coffee than they would if they took a scheduled break, and that may not be good for them, but that's another matter.)

What about temperature—can it play a significant role in determining whether or not one procrastinates?

Of course. Anything that causes discomfort provides additional temptation to postpone work, if one is so inclined; so to the extent that temperature can be controlled it's smart to do so.

A study several years ago at Johns Hopkins University[1] concluded that for physically strenuous work the optimum temperature is 60° Fahrenheit, for moderately hard physical work 65°. For desk work, the optimum varies with the seasons: the best winter temperature was found to be between 68° and 73°, and the best summer temperature between 75° and 80°.

But those are optimum temperatures, not required ones, and you shouldn't let a few degrees either side of the comfort zone serve as an excuse for procrastination. Just because you're a bit uncomfortable doesn't mean you can't work effectively. A little self-discipline can compensate for quite a few degrees on the thermometer.

Are there any other environmental factors that affect procrastination?

Yes. An important one is privacy. We've talked about various kinds of distractions, but there's no distraction quite so hard to deal with as other people. If the task you are procrastinating on is one that requires solitary effort, such as writing, researching, planning, and most other creative activities, you aren't apt to get much done until you solve the people problem. The mere fact that you know frequent interruptions *might* occur often precludes action, even though the interruptions themselves never materialize.

So try to give yourself some privacy, if you're facing the kind of task that requires it. At home, this may sometimes involve getting up a couple of hours earlier than the rest of the household, or staying up later, or making a deal with your spouse or children that you are to be incommunicado for a certain period.

Victor Hugo, the great French novelist, developed a rather drastic method of guaranteeing himself privacy. When he had periods of "writer's block" and was tempted to go for a walk, invite friends in, or visit a café instead of struggling with his manuscript, he fought the temptation by having his servant remove all of his clothes from the room, with instructions not to bring them back until a certain time. Sitting naked in his room, with nothing but pen, ink, and paper, there wasn't much left to do but sit down and write.

You may not want to go quite that far, but sometimes it can help to enlist the aid of someone else to assure the kind of environment where all temptation is removed.

But privacy is a little more difficult to achieve in the workplace than at home. If one works in a busy office, for example, how does one get any seclusion?

Well, to take the obvious first, if you happen to have a door on your office, don't become so enamored of the "open-door policy" that you leave it open all the time. By all means close it when you want to concentrate on a task. And have it understood by others in your workplace that the closed door is a signal that you prefer not to be disturbed by routine interruptions—but that it is not meant to screen out anything urgent. And when you close the door it sometimes helps to mention to your co-workers what it is you're going to be working on. If you've been procrastinating, or are tempted to, this process of secluding yourself for a specific purpose and announcing that you are doing so builds up psychological pressure to get the job done.

But most office workers don't have a private office, so they can't shut the door. What can they do?

Sometimes they can establish a greater feeling of privacy by simply placing their desk differently, so that they aren't facing a talkative co-worker or a busy corridor. Dividers or screens often can create a feeling of a private enclave. And the placement of file cabinets to establish territorial boundaries and to cut down on eye contact can be helpful.

You aren't saying that people should isolate themselves more, are you?

Not necessarily; some people need more interaction, not less. But if you procrastinate because of a feeling of being too much in a fishbowl, or if too-frequent interruptions make it difficult to carry a task to completion, the best answer may not be to grit your teeth and try harder but to find some way of getting a little more distance—physical or psychological— between you and other people.

One more thing needs to be said about the people problem. It isn't just a matter of how close or how distant people are from you: even more important is the question of what kind of people they are.

If you associate with doers, you tend to become more of a doer. If you associate with goof-offs, you tend to goof off. We absorb attitudes, emotions, and values from the people we are with. Perhaps the most important element in our environment is our associates.

That seems to imply that we are all like monkeys, imitating the behavior we observe around us. When people have a clear sense of their own priorities and values shouldn't they be able to withstand the adverse influence of associates who might tempt them to procrastinate? In other words, regardless of whom we associate with, shouldn't we all be "masters of our fates and captains of our souls"?

Character does, of course, insulate one to a considerable extent from adverse influences. But not completely. It's hard for even the most "self-actualized" person to maintain enthusiasm and dedication when continually in the presence of indifference. As someone has observed, "It's hard to soar with the eagles when you're among a bunch of turkeys!" Enthusiasm is contagious; so is lethargy. So one of the ways of demonstrating that you really *are* the "captain of your soul" is to chart a course that will carry you into different waters, where the climate is more conducive to action.

But that's easier said than done. In the workplace, especially, relationships are not a matter of choice. If you are part of a work crew, or if you are assigned to a particular office, your associates have been determined by the system and there isn't much you can do about it.

Granted, but you must do what you can. Your personal associations profoundly influence your life in many ways, not just in this matter of procrastination, and it is folly to establish relationships with people solely because of proximity, rather than on the basis of shared values and mutual concerns. In deciding whom to spend a coffee break with, or whom to go to lunch with, for example, remember that some people exude energy and vigor and others are wet blankets. By choosing the former whenever possible, you can establish a mutual support system from which you will both benefit.

Keep in mind also that associates occasionally may foster procrastination from ulterior motives. Jealousy or envy may cause them to entice you from work you should be doing, because they would rather see you become a little less effective. A spouse may become resentful of the time and interest you are investing in your career and may undermine your efforts, either consciously or unconsciously. When such situations exist, it is imperative that they be recognized for what they are so that the conflict can be discussed and resolved.

In summary, then, remember that procrastination is not always just an internal problem, a question of bad habits you may have acquired. It is influenced significantly by the surroundings in which you live and work, and there are many things you can do to modify your environment which will help you better to control your behavior. In other words, make sure that your battle with procrastination is being fought on terrain that favors you, not the enemy!

Taking the Seventh Step

Ask yourself to what extent your physical environment is dampening your efforts to get started on postponable tasks. Look around your office, your shop, your laboratory, your kitchen, or wherever it is that you do most of your work, and rate your environment on the following criteria:

	YES	NO
1. Is my work area reasonably orderly?	☐	☐
2. Do I have the tools and equipment I need?	☐	☐
3. Is my work area laid out with convenience in mind, so that the things used most often are easily accessible?	☐	☐
4. Do I have sufficient work space?	☐	☐
5. Is lighting adequate?	☐	☐
6. Are visible distractions kept to a minimum?	☐	☐
7. Is the noise level acceptable?	☐	☐
8. Do I have a good system for handling paperwork?	☐	☐
9. Can I maintain the temperature at a level conducive to work?	☐	☐
10. Do I have enough privacy to permit me to concentrate?	☐	☐

Keeping in mind that your inclination to act is either stimulated or stifled by your surroundings, ask yourself what, if anything, you can do about any item on the list to which you answered No.

When are you going to do it?

How about now?

Use the Reinforcement Principle

You have emphasized the power of self-discipline. But how do you make sure that when you discipline yourself to do something it isn't just a one-time thing? In other words, how do you build single actions into habit patterns, so that procrastination is less likely in the future?

You do it by using the principle of reinforcement.

Behavioral scientists have demonstrated that whenever a behavior occurs, the likelihood of it occurring again is strongly influenced by whatever happens *immediately afterward*. If the subsequent event is pleasant, the brain links the

117

two occurrences together. Even if the person is unaware of the linkage, the behavior is more likely to be repeated. The process is seen throughout the animal kingdom: it is a built-in mechanism that makes possible what psychologists call associative learning.

So if you want a particular action to be repeated, follow it immediately with a suitable reinforcer, some kind of reward that will have a positive effect. The reinforcer may be provided by someone else—as, for example, in the case of a football coach who gives a player a pat on the back after he has made an exceptional effort—or you can provide it for yourself, as when you give yourself some kind of reward for performing an unpleasant task you were tempted to postpone.

Wait a minute. You've warned against game playing. But aren't you playing games if you set up a system of rewarding yourself for desired behaviors?

Perhaps it could be called that. But games can serve a purpose, and this one certainly does, so I see nothing wrong with it.

But the game seems rather pointless, anyway, because when you reward yourself it's like taking something out of one pocket and putting it in the other. Aren't you robbing Peter to pay Paul?

If Peter doesn't mind, and if it makes Paul happy, why not? Self-reward costs nothing, provides proven benefits, and is little trouble—so isn't it worth trying?

But some people would argue that it's demeaning to "bribe" yourself to do something that you know you should do anyway. Shouldn't the satisfaction of a job well-done be reward enough?

It often is. For many people the knowledge that they will earn self-satisfaction is sufficient motivation to get them to perform a distasteful task at the appropriate time. Such people have learned to utilize the most important reinforcer of all and are to be commended—if everyone were like them there would be no such thing as procrastination, a book like this one would never be written, and it would be a much different world. But many people aren't like that; they doubt they can do the job satisfactorily, or they are immobilized by anticipation of discomfort, or by shyness, or by fear of success, or by one of the other inhibitors we've talked about, so they postpone action. Such people may find it's necessary to sweeten the pot by providing some additional rewards.

This can hardly be referred to as bribery, because that word implies something improper. After all, what's wrong with being rewarded? Welders and teachers and physicians do their work partly because of the satisfaction they get from doing it—but they usually don't continue very long unless that intrinsic reward is supplemented by some additional reinforcement, such as a paycheck, recognition, or benefits.

Those examples aren't quite the same. What you are advocating involves giving oneself a reward, instead of earning one from an outside source.

It doesn't matter. The psychological lift—in other words, the reinforcement—that you get from rewarding yourself can sometimes be even more effective than one bestowed by someone else.

In a program designed to improve study skills, some university students were divided into three groups. In one group—the control group—participants were encouraged to improve their study habits, but no reward system was established. Members of the second group could earn back a ten-dollar deposit through a self-administered program, based on each student's own self-evaluation of his or her progress. Those in the third group also put up a ten-dollar deposit, which could be earned back based on a combination of a group leader's evaluation and externally administered rewards. Both the second and third groups outperformed the first; a follow-up study four months later indicated that those in the self-administered-reward group continued to improve their study habits substantially more than those who had received externally determined rewards.[1]

Another study involved students who indicated they had serious problems in one or more of four areas: eating, smoking, studying, or dating. Of the various methods of behavior change used by the successful students, self-reward was the most popular and most successful in each of the four problem areas.[2]

And granting (or withholding) the rewards yourself is especially advantageous if the problem you are dealing with is a habit such as procrastination.

Why is that?

First, procrastination is a very subjective thing. The line between goofing off and legitimate delay is often a fine one, and nobody is in as good a position as you to serve as a judge.

Second, if you plan to reinforce many small steps, instead of just earning a reward for a major achievement, the process becomes a nuisance for the other person and therefore tends not to work over a prolonged period. Remember, that other person isn't nearly as motivated as you are to see that the program is followed.

Third, and most important of all, it's a shame to put control of your behavior into the hands of someone else, thereby acknowledging and reinforcing your own weakness, immaturity, and lack of self-discipline. The more independent you become of other people—including friends, co-workers, and family—the more self-esteem you build. You were not put on this earth to curry the approval of others. Your foremost goal should be to earn the respect of the person you see in the mirror every day; all else is secondary.

You see, what we're talking about here concerns attitudes rather than logic. It's true that with self-reinforcement you aren't earning your reward in the same sense as a worker is earning a paycheck; you have it within your power to obtain it simply by cheating, or by changing the rules, or by "forgetting," so it's not a true contingency. But the mind doesn't make that distinction; it merely links the unpleasant task with the pleasant consequence, and from then on the task becomes a little less formidable, a little more palatable. And procrastination becomes a little less likely.

But what about the temptation to cheat? If you don't have enough willpower to do the job without reinforcement, what's to prevent you from giving yourself the reinforcement without earning it?

That's always a possibility, and if it happens you'll have to try another gambit. But most people don't cheat. Having gone to the trouble of establishing the contingency, and having made a deal with themselves, they generally make a sincere effort to keep the bargain. After all, there's no point in cheating yourself!

Do you recommend keeping a written record of how well you're doing?

Most of the research on behavior modification involves meticulous record-keeping in order to measure the success rate. If you are dealing with an easily measured behavior, such as how often you have done your quota of calisthenics, or how many pages you have written each day on your master's thesis, then that's the scientific way to go about it. But most people are turned off by the nuisance of recording their behavior, and the kinds of things we procrastinate on don't always lend themselves to easy graphing. So experiment. If keeping a written record isn't too much bother, you'll probably find it helpful; on the other hand, if it turns out to be an unacceptable chore, just remember that it isn't essential.

Your purpose is to shape your behavior, not to obtain data for scholarly research. You'll know whether or not you're making progress.

Suppose a person does decide to keep a written record. What kind do you recommend?

A cumulative graph is generally the best bet.

Why?

Let's take that master's thesis as an example You've been procrastinating but finally resolve to get started on it, and you set a goal of writing four pages a day. You spend as much time on it each day as you can, but the number of pages you actually produce is:

Monday	3
Tuesday	2
Wednesday	4
Thursday	0
Friday	2

You've written a total of eleven pages during the week, but as you look at the figures you're disheartened. Only one day out of the five did you reach your goal. That's failure. It's discouraging. Your enthusiasm wanes and procrastination sets in again.

If you were to convert your figures to a bar graph, it would look like this:

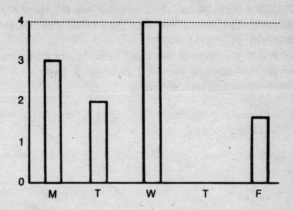

The effect is still discouraging, perhaps even more so. There's a big gap between those bars and the dotted line that represents your daily goal. If you were to put the data on a line graph the result would be no better:

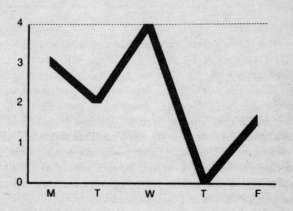

Still a bleak picture. Not only did you fall short of your goal four days out of five, but the overall trend is clearly downward. A gloomy thought.

But if you were to put those same figures on a cumulative graph—showing the total number of pages you have written—it would look like this:

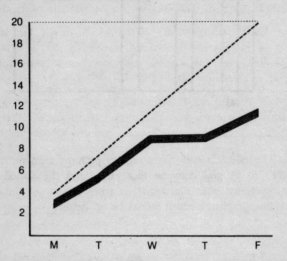

It is still apparent that you didn't do what you had hoped to do (represented by the dotted line), but you've accomplished quite a bit. You can see how much better off you are than when the week began, and you give yourself a mental pat on the back. Not too generous a pat—after all, you didn't make that line as steep as you had hoped, and procrastination did rear its ugly head on Thursday—but you're nevertheless looking at a picture of solid achievement, and you can see that you're moving toward your goal. The other graphs are accurate, but psychologically they are downers. This one gives you a psychological boost.

It seems almost as if you're so desperate to make things look good that you're willing to manipulate the data a little, instead of facing the cold, hard truth.

Not at all. There's nothing untrue or deceptive about that cumulative graph. It's simply a matter of viewing the truth in the best light. You're just accentuating the positive.

Well, perhaps. But you'll have to admit that during the weeks and months ahead, assuming that the present rate continues, the gap between your cumulative achievement and your cumulative goal is going to get pretty wide.

That brings up another point. In view of what happened during the week, I think that in this case, whether you use a graph or not, you should consider adjusting your goal downward. Of course, if your failure to meet your quota was a result of goofing off, then you should leave your goal at four, and get off your duff. But if you really worked hard on Monday, Tuesday, and Friday and still were able to do only two or three pages on those days, then I'd be inclined to go back to the drawing board and establish three pages, or even two and a half, as the goal.

You want an objective that you have a good chance of reaching on a typical day, not one that represents a rare achievement. Otherwise you deprive yourself of the opportunity for reinforcement.

Now you really are manipulating the rules! You're like a tennis player who keeps hitting the ball into the net, then lowers the net to correct the problem!

I realize that it looks that way, but nevertheless it makes sense.

Let's use a different sport as our analogy. Suppose you are a high jumper whose hope is to clear seven feet, but you can clear only six. You don't gain anything by bravely leaving the bar at seven feet and knocking it off on every jump. You're better off to lower it to six, then raise it gradually if and when your skill and your confidence warrant it.

It's the same with our thesis example. The four-page goal was set arbitrarily, based on hope rather than experience. It isn't sacred; it is simply a figure you picked as an aid to overcoming inertia. If, instead, it proves so difficult to attain regularly that it causes discouragement, it has become part of the problem rather than part of the solution. So adjust it. The reinforcement technique can't work unless you have a few successes to reinforce!

What kinds of rewards make the best reinforcers?

Anything pleasurable will work. It can be something intangible, such as giving yourself permission to do something you feel like doing—a walk around the block, for example, or a rest, or a brief chat with someone—or it can be something tangible, such as a drink of water, a candy bar, or a cup of coffee. Smokers find that a cigarette can be a powerful reinforcer, so if you happen to have the smoking habit here's one way you may be able to get some benefit from it!

One researcher, Dr. David Premack, demonstrated that any activity that a person tends to do frequently in a free situation (brushing one's hair, stretching, chewing gum, reading the newspaper, putting on makeup, snacking, socializing, etc.) can be used as a reinforcer, even though one might not think of it as especially rewarding. Thus we have what behaviorists call the Premack Principle: *Given two behaviors of different probabilities, the more probable behavior can be used to reinforce the less probable.*[3]

So opportunities for reinforcement are around us all the time. By forming the habit of using as contingencies the myriad little things we often do anyway, we can steadily shape our behavior along the lines we desire.

When we fail to do this, undesired behaviors often become entrenched because of their own intrinsic reinforcers. The reason procrastination is so universal and so deeply ingrained is that it is automatically encouraged by the very process we have been talking about: an act of procrastination is invariably followed by immediate reinforcement.

Suppose, for example, that a student decides to postpone some urgent homework, turning on the television instead. The decision to postpone is followed by an instant reward, namely, amusement and the avoidance of something difficult. The ultimate penalty for this decision—the pain of staying up all night to get the assignment done, or the acceptance of a lower grade in the course—may far outweigh the fleeting reward in the final analysis, *but because the penalty isn't immediate, the undesired behavior is nevertheless reinforced.*

So if we are to achieve self-mastery, distant goals and distant rewards must be supplemented by intermediate goals and immediate rewards.

You keep talking about rewards. What about the other side of the coin? Can't punishments be as useful as rewards in a self-administered program of behavior change?

As a general rule, no. There must be penalties, of course, in the sense of withholding the reward if the desired behavior doesn't occur; but to inflict pain or discomfort on yourself deliberately as punishment for having failed to measure up is generally ineffective.

But what about the analogy of using both the carrot and the stick to get the mule to move? Shouldn't the same principle work with people? Can't we motivate ourselves with both the carrot and the stick?

127

Most psychologists caution that this is unwise, especially in a self-administered program. Your punishment should be simply depriving yourself of the carrot. Forget about the stick.

Psychologists have a term for the stick. They call it "aversive conditioning," and it is sometimes used in treatment of certain behavior disorders—but usually with someone else enforcing the punishment.

Occasionally this does work for procrastination. For example, suppose you want to go on a diet, but just can't get started. Suppose also that your husband likes to smoke cigars, but you have an agreement with him that he won't smoke in the house, because you detest the smell. You might hand him an envelope containing enough cash to buy a box of his favorite cigars, and give him permission to smoke all of them in the house if you haven't lost ten pounds by a certain date, with the understanding that if you have, the money will be returned to you. By putting the enforcement of your contract into the hands of someone else, you increase the probability that the penalty will be enforced and that the contract therefore will be effective.

But this sort of ploy is usually a one-time thing. For establishing more general habit patterns, for shaping behavior so as to consistently avoid procrastination of all kinds, rewards have been found to be a much stronger motivator than avoidance of punishment.

What about the times when one has earned a reward but nothing seems handy at the moment as a reinforcer?

A mental pat on the back can be a powerful reinforcer. When you've taken a step toward the completion of that task you've been putting off, praise yourself mentally. Relish your accomplishment. Lay it on thick—you need all the encouragement you can get, and if you don't provide it nobody will.

And remember, just as the pessimist sees the glass as

half empty while the optimist sees it as half full, so your effort often can be considered either a failure or a success, depending on your point of view. Suppose you resolved to clean three rooms of your house today but were able to do only one. You can consider that a failure, new proof of your ineptitude and laziness—in which case you will feel discouraged, and procrastination is likely to set in again. Or you can say to yourself, "I may have fallen short of my goal, but I accomplished *something*, and I can take comfort in that. I proved that I could at least make a start. I'm that much closer to my goal than when the day began." Now your mood is positive, and further procrastination is less likely. *By reinforcing whatever gains you made, however small, you have established a base on which to build.*

You can't always avoid failure, but you can always control your reaction to failure. And one way to do so is to reinforce—either overtly or mentally—every slight movement in the right direction.

When the reinforcement process fails, what is usually the reason?

It's usually because of making the reward contingent on reaching a distant or overambitious goal, rather than an immediate and modest one.

For example, suppose you are procrastinating putting your garden in, which you figure is about a five-hour job. Don't say to yourself, "If I finish the garden today I'll reward myself tonight with a steak dinner." Instead, say, "As soon as I get my work clothes on and haul that bag of peat moss to the garden, I'll give myself permission to pause and eat that apple I'm in the mood for."

That apple may be the only reinforcer you'll need, because once you get started your momentum will probably carry you through—in which case you won't have to worry about rewarding yourself for subsequent phases of your gardening project. In other words, the apple, used this way, can be a more powerful reinforcer than the steak dinner!

The law of inertia is at work here: your big problem is that being at rest you tend to remain at rest. Once enough incentive has been provided just to get you started, momentum will usually see you through. Don't hesitate to reward yourself for tiny steps or for working on something for just five minutes.

Then you recommend making a contract with yourself mainly in connection with initiating a task, rather than in connection with completing it?

In the case of a large task, yes. The tiny but immediate reward for taking an initial step or a small incremental step is more effective as a self-administered motivator than a generous reward that can be earned only after prolonged effort. But keep in mind that it's not an either/or proposition. You can use incremental rewards *and* completion rewards, so why not do so? Why not set up a lavish self-compensation program, if that's what it takes? I dare say you can't think of a more deserving person than yourself—especially after you will have resolutely completed that distasteful task ahead of schedule! So don't be stingy. Having demonstrated your iron will, your sterling character, your total self-mastery, you've earned a few perks!

Someone has said that one of the secrets of a happy life is never to stifle a generous impulse. Surely that applies to being generous with yourself as well as with others—provided you are being generous in rewarding performance, not delay.

Taking the Eighth Step

From one of your four lists select a task you've been post-poning that you would like to get done right now. Break it down into small increments: if you were going to do it, what would be the first step? The second? The third?

Now ask yourself, "What am I in the mood for right now—some little thing that I can easily grant myself, such as a stretch break, a snack, a chat, a drink, a game of cards, a face-wash, a change of clothes, a favorite recording?"

Tell yourself you may claim that reward as soon as you take the first small step toward completion of your task, at which time you will figure out ways to reward yourself for subsequent steps or for completing the task. (And don't forget to supplement your reinforcement with one of the most important reinforcers of all—lavish self-congratulation for having finally taken action on a nagging chore.)

You really are in the mood for that reward, aren't you? Okay, go ahead and earn it.

Now!

Consider Deliberate Delay

You keep talking about procrastination as if it were always bad. But aren't there times when it pays to procrastinate?

Not if you define procrastination as I do, which is the postponement of something that you know you really should be doing.

However, if you use the word the way some people do, meaning simply to put something off until a future time, then of course there are times when it is justified. In those cases it might be more appropriate to refer to it as deliberate delay. (I've also seen it referred to as purposeful procrastination, positive procrastination, prudent postponement, watchful waiting, and discerning disregard.*)

One master of deliberate delay was the Roman general Quintus Fabius, whose tactics earned him the nickname Cunctator, meaning procrastinator, or delayer.

When the victorious army of Hannibal swept across Spain and France, and over the Alps into northern Italy, Fabius was given the task of defeating him. But realizing that Hannibal had a lot going for him—momentum, battle-seasoned troops, high morale, and tactical genius—Fabius simply kept postponing the expected clash between his army and the Carthaginian invaders. Instead, he continually harassed Hannibal's army, attacking stragglers, cutting convoys, feinting and dodging, forever delaying the major battle that Hannibal—and the citizens of Rome—expected at any moment. In the meantime, Hannibal's supplies were running low and his soldiers were feeling more and more frustrated.

Did the citizens of Rome appreciate the wisdom of this "deliberate delay"?

No, they decided that Fabius was either a coward or a procrastinator. So they replaced him, and with an overwhelming force of 86,000 men and 6,000 horses the Romans attacked Hannibal's 50,000-man army at Cannae. What followed, as every schoolboy knows, was one of the great battles of history.

In case any schoolboy may have forgotten, how did it turn out? Did the Romans win?

No, they got clobbered. Hannibal outsmarted them, yielding the center of his line, then attacking from both sides.**

---

* A prime prerequisite for writing on this subject, it would seem, is a pronounced propensity for apt alliteration.

** The draw play, obviously, was not invented on the football field.

The Romans were bunched together so closely that they couldn't use their weapons or their horses effectively, and by the end of the battle—or, more accurately, the massacre—there were 70,000 dead or wounded Roman soldiers left on the field and thousands taken prisoner. Only a handful escaped to return to Rome.

At that point, the Romans decided that perhaps Fabius Cuncator's plan of "deliberate delay" hadn't been such a bad idea after all. They restored him to power and returned to his policy of avoiding further head-on clashes with Hannibal as long as possible. Meanwhile they were able to regroup and launch an assault in North Africa on Carthage itself.

Hannibal is supposed to have been one of the great military geniuses of all time. What prevented him from marching on to Rome after the Cannae victory, and capturing it to become the ruler of the known world?

Procrastination.

Of course, Hannibal gave himself a lot of good reasons for not following up on his victory: his troops were battle-weary, winter was approaching, he needed siege boats, he had reason to believe that several of Rome's allies might desert Rome and join him, and so on. But later, he is said to have admitted that he made a great mistake in not striking promptly, exploiting the disarray of the Romans. If he had done so, the history of the world would have been quite different.

But it seems that there are two conflicting lessons to be learned from this example. Fabius deliberately delayed confronting the enemy, and you say this was wise; Hannibal deliberately delayed attacking Rome, and you say this was a mistake.

True. Delay is in itself neither good nor bad: it depends upon the circumstances and the reasons. Both of these generals were practicing purposeful procrastination, as distinguished from the kind we've been talking about in preceding chapters. They postponed action—but for what they believed to be valid reasons. In the case of Fabius, events proved him right; in the case of Hannibal, they didn't. But both were postponing on the basis of their considered judgment, rather than because of self-deception, laziness, timidity, indecision, indifference, distraction, or the other reasons we've discussed.

So deliberate delay is no assurance that you're doing the right thing—your judgment may or may not prove sound—but at least you're not guilty of putting off something you know you should do now.

But always remember the main lesson to be learned from the experience of Hannibal: the importance of moving swiftly to exploit a victory or an accomplishment while you have momentum. Success breeds success—but only when mated with prompt action.

Are there other situations in which deliberate delay should be considered?

Yes, there are several. One is when additional information is needed in order to act wisely. But remember that the dividing line between indecision and deliberate delay is a fine one, and the temptation is to use lack of information as a cop-out, so force yourself to consider these four questions:

1. Do you *really* need more facts? Isn't additional information likely to confirm what you already know?
2. How much risk is actually involved in going ahead with the facts you have now? Keeping in mind that delay also has risks, and that fortune favors the bold, shouldn't you gamble on action rather than inaction?
3. Assuming that you really do need more facts before

going ahead, are you doing everything you can to get them promptly, instead of just waiting for them to drift in?

4. Are you succumbing to the vice of perfectionism, insisting on an answer to every conceivable objection before deciding to act? If so, remember Patton's law: A good plan today is worth more than a perfect plan tomorrow.

Some people claim that procrastination is justified because problems sometimes solve themselves if left alone. Isn't this true?

Yes, sometimes it is. It's the exception, but it does happen, and in certain circumstances you might want to consider deliberate delay on these grounds. (But remember that problems that go away by themselves often come back by themselves, so be sure you're not fooling yourself.)

Napoleon is said to have consciously followed this policy, putting all routine letters aside for two weeks before replying to them. He claimed that during that period most matters had taken care of themselves; those that had not, he could now handle in a more leisurely manner.[1] (On the other hand, whenever time was critical Napoleon moved swiftly. "The reason I defeated the Austrians," he once said, "is because they did not understand the value of five minutes.")

You aren't suggesting that people should follow Napoleon's example and delay answering letters for a couple of weeks, are you?

Ordinarily, no. If you definitely intend to answer a letter, and know what your answer will be, you should reply immediately. No question about it. In fact, if I were to recommend a military leader as a model of organizational efficiency, instead of Napoleon I think I would select General George C.

Marshall, whom Winston Churchill described as "the organizer of victory." Marshall made it a rule to answer every letter, memo, or note on the day it was received.[2] I wouldn't argue that his avoidance of procrastination was the principal factor in Marshall's administrative brilliance, but it was certainly significant. And the self-discipline it involves is an essential ingredient of character.

On the other hand, I think that with letter-writing or any other activity, there sometimes are benefits to be gained by watchful waiting, and I don't consider that to be procrastination. I think it's more aptly described by the phrase, "benign neglect." Fiddling with a problem may do more harm than good; ignoring it and letting nature take its course is sometimes smarter.

Often, though, it's more than just leaving something alone. Often the purpose is to give an idea time to incubate.

Incubate? You mean like an egg?

Yes.

But your analogy is faulty. An egg incubates because the embryo is getting a steady supply of warmth, which it needs to develop. With an idea, though, if you put it aside and think about something else, it's as if it were in deep freeze. Nothing's happening to it.

At a conscious level, that's true. But the subconscious mind may be keeping that embryonic idea warm. All sorts of development may be taking place, even though you're unaware of it.

Everyone has had the experience of wrestling with a problem without success, when suddenly, while one is involved in some unrelated activity, the solution will present itself out of the blue. It's apparent, in such cases, that the subconscious mind has been mulling the matter over while the conscious mind was otherwise engaged. Instead of just allowing this to happen on a chance basis, it pays sometimes to consign a problem deliberately to a period of incubation.

Henry J. Kaiser, the founder of the Kaiser Corporation, regularly used this technique. He maintained that his subconscious mind often was most effective while he was asleep, and he made it a habit before retiring each night to pause a moment and reflect about the most important problem he was going to have to deal with the next day. Then he would put it out of his mind and go to sleep. Often he would have a solution to the problem—or at least a different perspective on it—when he awoke. Many people in time management seminars have told me they do the same thing. So this idea of assigning an idea to the subconscious to "incubate" does work—for some people, at least.

But you said earlier that indecision is one form of procrastination, and is a bad habit. Anyone doing what you've just suggested certainly isn't being decisive; aren't you contradicting yourself?

I don't think so. There are two basic types of decisions. One is choosing from among two or more clear-cut alternatives, where the pros and cons are evident, and it's a simple weighing process: Should I buy the blue suit or the brown one? Should I rent or buy? Should I go by plane or by car?

These decisions usually should be made without undue delay, I think, after the relevant facts have been considered, and once made should be put behind you. You shouldn't spend time and energy agonizing over whether the decision was the right one. Unless new facts come to light you should put the matter out of your mind and concentrate on other things.

The other type of decision is the unstructured kind, where instead of choosing from alternatives you are asking open-ended questions, such as: Am I considering all the possible options? What would be a creative way of dealing with this dilemma? Why do I feel uneasy about this situation?

Those questions—the kind that seem to call for creative responses—are the ones that justify incubation. And incubation should not be thought of as indecision or procrastination.

Of course, sometimes the purpose of delay is not to keep something "warm," but just the opposite—to permit cooling off. Would that be considered another legitimate excuse for delay?

Indeed it would. Postponing action that might be based on emotion rather than on considered judgment is not procrastination.

After Benjamin Franklin's death, there was found among his papers a draft of a letter he had angrily written in 1775 to his close friend, William Strahan, upon learning that Strahan had voted in Parliament against the interests of the American colonies. It read:

> Mr. Strahan:
>   You are a member of Parliament, and one of that majority which has doomed my country to destruction. You have begun to burn our towns and murder our people. Look upon your hands! They are stained with the blood of your relations. You and I were long friends. You are now my enemy, and I am
>
> Yours,
B. Franklin

The letter was never sent. Two days later, after some "deliberate delay," Franklin had cooled off and recognized that such a biting letter would accomplish nothing. He wrote another letter to Strahan—a strong one, pointing out that "words and arguments are now of no use," but without the asperity of his first draft, thus avoiding a rupture in their lifelong friendship and an end to all communication.[3]

Sometimes deliberate delay is useful not to give yourself a cooling-off period, but to provide one for someone else. For example, President John F. Kennedy, furious over a Huntley-Brinkley report critical of his administration, once ordered Newton Minow, chairman of the Federal Communications Commission, to do whatever he could to punish NBC. As related by Ross Webber, "Mr. Minow did nothing, then wrote Kennedy indicating how lucky he was to have subordinates too loyal to always do as they were told." Kennedy, whose anger had now abated, of course agreed.[4]

Aside from the reasons we have discussed thus far for deliberate delay, there is another: to stimulate learning. It has been found that a single intensive period of study is a less effective way of learning than spending the same amount of time spread out over an extended period.

You commented earlier on the importance of concentration. Doesn't this contradict that principle?

In a way, yes. It's an exception. Concentration pays big dividends up to a certain point, but beyond that point mental fatigue diminishes effectiveness, especially in the learning process.

In one demonstration of this effect, three different groups of research subjects were given a difficult task: copying a complex design while seeing the pencil and paper only in a mirror. One group used a massed learning approach, performing the task twenty times without a pause. The second group was given a minute's rest between drawings, the third a day's rest. Those who had a day's rest—"distributed practice"—performed much better than the other groups. The poorest performance was by the group that had used the massed approach.[5]

Cramming for an exam, as many students have found, can produce dramatic—but usually short-lived—results. A better way, if you want the information to stick with you, is to use the technique of spaced repetition.

You've discussed the value of deliberate delay from the standpoint of the individual. Does the same principle apply with groups?

Indeed it does. Even more so, because groups, especially large ones, tend to act impetuously, swayed by a felicitous phrase or an emotional outburst. Getting an assembly to suspend judgment on a matter that has not been adequately analyzed should be thought of as prudence, not procrastination.

Techniques have been developed in recent years for structuring problem-solving meetings to postpone criticism and evaluation of ideas until after every idea the group can come up with—good or bad—has been presented. An outgrowth of the brainstorming technique developed by advertising executive Alex Osborne three decades ago, this somewhat ritualized method of deliberate delay has been found useful in preventing groups from jumping to conclusions and going off half-cocked under the guise of avoiding procrastination.[6]

Are there any other uses of deliberate delay, aside from those you've mentioned?

One other that you might find useful is a technique suggested by time management expert Alan Lakein, which he calls "procrastinating positively." He claims that when all other methods for coping with procrastination fail, it can be helpful just to make yourself sit in a chair and do nothing. No reading, no talking, no paperwork, no knitting, no TV, just sit completely still for fifteen or twenty minutes. Meanwhile, that important task that you should be doing is staring you in the face, and you realize how your precious time is slipping away. "Whenever I find myself procrastinating, this is the technique I use," Lakein says. "Believe me, after ten minutes I'm off and running . . ."[7]

If it's possible to fight fire with fire, perhaps it's possible to fight procrastination with procrastination. As a last resort, you may find this system worth a try.

Taking the Ninth Step

Look over your four lists and ask yourself whether you have included some things that don't belong there—things you're not really procrastinating on, but that you are deferring for very good reasons.

Be careful. Keep in mind that overuse of this procedure of justifying delay is what causes a large portion of your (and the world's) problems, so give each item a rigorous examination.

Having identified any that may qualify for that coveted designation of Deliberate Delay, cross them off your procrastination lists. But don't just let it go at that. Establish a timetable for action on those items. Give yourself a deadline for taking them off the back burner, and note that deadline on your calendar or in your tickler file.

This process serves two purposes: it forces you to crystallize your thinking about these tasks, to determine which category they really belong in and why; and it leaves you feeling differently about the things still on your lists. No longer can you tell yourself that some of them can be postponed in good conscience, because everything in that category has been removed. Each item on the list now is an example of stark, unmitigated procrastination, and you have no choice but to face up to that fact and stop kidding yourself.

So go over your lists and extract any items that don't belong there. Then if you neglect them further you can say you're doing it "benignly."

Do it now.

Manage Your Time

You've talked a lot about procrastination resulting from such things as fear, indecision, fatigue, unpleasantness, lack of self-discipline, and so on, but you've said nothing about what some people would consider the most common cause of all.

What's that?

Lack of time. The reason something is postponed often has nothing to do with any mental block—it's just that there's no time available. So we have what might be called unavoidable procrastination.

Unavoidable procrastination? That sounds like a term invented by someone looking for an excuse to goof off.

Well, what else can you call it? If you have more to do than you can possibly get done, something's got to give. Some of those activities, no matter how much you'd like to do them, must be postponed. Call it what you will, delay is unavoidable. And since this happens every day in the lives of millions of people, there's a lot of unavoidable procrastination going on.

There's a lot of procrastination going on, that's for sure, but before we call it unavoidable let's take a closer look. What kinds of activities are you talking about?

Simple things, like pruning the roses, grooming the dog, fixing the lamp switch, organizing the bookshelves, getting a haircut, having the brakes adjusted, building a birdhouse, playing volleyball at the Y, defrosting the refrigerator, reading Huckleberry Finn, *playing the piano, shining some shoes—the list is endless. Things you genuinely want to get to, either because they're fun or because you'd like to get them taken care of, but there just aren't enough hours in the day. So you put them off. What else can you do?*

Plenty.

First, before we talk about pruning the roses, let's talk about pruning our list. Look it over carefully, item by item, and ask if there aren't some things that could be crossed off, not because they are worthless or undesirable but because in view of the limitations of time and the relatively minor satisfaction they provide they should be eliminated to make way for something else.

That's a cheap shot, if you'll permit a candid observation. The question we're considering is, "How do you do

all these things?" And you respond by saying, "Just don't."
Not very helpful!

Be patient—we'll find time for those that matter, but first we want to make sure that they really *do* matter. Let's face it—it's possible to bite off more than you can chew, to assign yourself more things than can possibly be done. Some-one has said that when people pray, they are usually saying, in effect, "Please, God, fix it so that just this once two plus two will equal five!" That's what you're doing when you say, "I want to do more in twenty-four hours than can be done in twenty-four hours. Show me how." Well, I'll show you how to do the things that are really important to you, but the first step is to eliminate those that aren't.

For example, looking over the list you just gave, suppose you decide that everything on the list is unquestionably worth devoting time to—except maybe the birdhouse. You decide that instead of building the birdhouse maybe you could buy one. Or talk your kid into making one. Or pay the boy next door to build you one. Or perhaps just forget the whole thing and let the birds fend for themselves.

When you cross off that item you've accomplished two things: you no longer have the guilty feeling that you're procrastinating on that birdhouse project, and you have eliminated the possibility that you might spend an hour building a birdhouse when the time would have been better spent pruning the roses or fixing the lamp.

So you're saying that it's important to establish priorities.

No, it's more than that. You're establishing what Peter Drucker calls "posteriorities," identifying those things that should not just be shuffled around on your list but should be removed from it entirely. That's much harder to do, but it's the only way you can simplify your life. Otherwise you're nagged eternally by conflicting and unrealistic demands on your time.

Okay, so we've located a "posteriority"—the bird-house—and eliminated it. That still leaves us with lots of tasks on the back burner. What's next?

We talked earlier about the fact that many chores can be classified either as important or as urgent—or both. But there are some that are neither, yet need to be done. They don't loom very large in the grand scheme of things, and there's no pressure to get them done immediately—but they can't be ignored. After all, if you devote time only to matters of cosmic importance, you'll go through life without ever clipping your toenails! So we have the problem of taking care of the "housekeeping" activities: the cleaning, mending, fixing, oiling, grooming, tidying, organizing, and so on. Or, in the workplace, doing the routine paperwork.

Many chores of that kind are automatically handled on an ad hoc basis, of course, just filling in odd moments. But procrastination usually keeps some of them forever on the back burner. When that happens, your best bet is simply to schedule a block of time, well in advance, to be allocated to that chore: "Saturday morning I'm going to clean out the attic," or "Tuesday evening I'm going to organize my recipe file," or "every Friday afternoon I'm going to catch up on my expense report and my filing."

So you're saying that one way to get these things done is simply to plan to do them. That's not an especially profound idea!

Profundity is not what we're concerned with. We're concerned with what works.

Look: the reason Mr. Jones has not cleaned out his attic for the past five years, even though he's been "meaning to get around to it" all that time, is that never once during

147

those five years has he said to himself, "Next Saturday morning is attic-cleaning time. I'm not going to go shopping, I'm not going to work in the yard, I'm not going to sleep late— I'm going to clean out that damned attic."

This solution to the problem may not seem dramatic or innovative, but it gets the attic cleaned out. What more can you ask?

Okay. But suppose a person has done the things you've mentioned, but still finds there aren't enough hours in the day to do everything that seems worth doing. Any further suggestions?

Yes, indeed. You may not be able to increase the number of hours in the day, but there are things that can be done to use the available hours more effectively, freeing up time for other things.* Everyone drifts into inefficient practices that gobble up lots of time, without any compensating benefit in terms of achievement, relaxation, or anything else. If we can establish more efficient habits we can recapture time that can then be reallocated to such things as the roses, the dog, the lamp, and all the rest. That could go a long way toward solving the problem of "not enough hours."

Would it really, though? Efficiency is fine, but how much time could a person actually gain?

Well, it's impossible to quantify, of course, but in my seminars I promise people they will pick up at least two hours a day by practicing the principles of effective time management. That must be a fairly reasonable figure—I've made that promise to thousands of people, and so far none have told me they followed my suggestions and they didn't work.

* For a more extensive treatment of this subject, see *Getting Things Done: The ABC's of Time Management*, by Edwin C. Bliss (New York: Charles Scribner's Sons, 1976; paperback 1983).

Two extra hours a day admittedly would make quite a dent in anybody's list of untackled tasks. How does one go about it?

The first principle to understand is that you will never be effective if you go through life "playing it by ear," always just doing whatever seems most important or most urgent at the time. You must plan far enough ahead that the exigencies of the moment are not nipping at your heels, distracting you from long-range considerations.

Toward the end of each week sit down with a pencil and paper—or with your desk calendar, your personal computer, or other scheduling device—and do some planning for the upcoming week. And don't just plan events—plan *activities* as well.

Would you give an example of what you mean by that?

Sure. Suppose you are an office worker. You sit down on Friday afternoon and make your schedule for the coming week, which looks like this:

Monday

9 to 9:30 A.M.	Attend staff meeting
Noon	Lunch with Jim and Sue
3 P.M.	See Robertson

Tuesday

8:30 A.M.	Leave car for tune-up
11 A.M.	Attend departmental planning conference
2 P.M.	Attend personnel committee meeting
5:15 P.M.	Pick up car

Wednesday

10:30 A.M.	Dental appointment
Noon	Luncheon club meets
2 to 5 P.M.	Monthly visit to branch office

Thursday

10 A.M.	Attend computer orientation briefing
Noon	Lunch with boss
	Budget due today

Friday

9:30 A.M.	Meet with Williams
	Copy for brochure due at printer
	Weekly report due

That schedule is typical of the "planning" most people do. I don't consider that planning at all. It's better than nothing, I suppose, but it isn't sufficient. You're not controlling your time.

Why not? Admittedly the schedule doesn't contain a lot of detail, but it contains the essentials. If you put in too much detail you don't have the flexibility to adapt to unforeseen events.

More detail isn't what we're after. The problem with that schedule is that it lists only *events*—appointments, meetings, and deadlines. No thought has been given to such questions as, "What should I focus on next week in order to move me toward my goals? What major things should I be concerned with that will benefit my department? What should I be doing to further my career? What future problems can I avoid by scheduling some preliminary work next week, thereby gaining lead time? What are the things that nobody has assigned me to do next week, but that I should assign myself to do, because they really matter?"

In other words, in preparing that schedule you've done a good job of *listing*, but a poor job of *planning*. You've established where you're going to be at certain times on certain days, but you've given no thought to what you really want to accomplish on those days. You've constructed a skeleton; now you need to put some flesh on the bones.

So if I were to suggest improvements in that schedule they would not consist of more minutiae, nor would I recommend filling in all the blank spaces; what I would recommend is that you plan to spend at least one substantial block of time each day working on some important but not urgent task (the urgent ones seem to get taken care of automatically). Some of these may be suggested by the items already listed: for example, perhaps it would be wise to block out time Monday afternoon to work on that brochure copy that is going to be due Friday; maybe some time should be scheduled early in the week to work on that budget that must be submitted Thursday; perhaps a little time should be scheduled prior to the conferences with Robertson and Williams, and prior to the meetings and the branch office visit, to do some preliminary spadework. In other words, schedule thinking time and working time as well as meeting time.

Besides the things suggested by your list of deadlines and appointments, there will be other matters that should be assigned specific time periods: projects you've been putting off, opportunities you've been meaning to take advantage of, planning you've intended to do. Just because these things don't involve deadlines doesn't mean that they should be carried around in your head in the hope that sometime you'll remember to get around to them. Put them in writing—and assign them a time slot—or they'll wind up in limbo.

What other principles of time management are of particular significance?

I believe you will markedly enhance your effectiveness if you will try to steer clear of the following ten vices: floundering, wheelspinning, fire fighting, vacillating, dawdling, spraying, switching, acquiescing, rehashing, and perfecting. Avoid those errors and I guarantee you'll gain enough time every day to do most of the things on your so-called "unavoidable procrastination" list.

Would you explain what you mean by each of those terms?

Okay, let's start with "floundering." By that I mean that many people fail to focus their efforts in a single direction. The reason usually is that they don't have clear-cut goals in mind, so they don't establish any momentum toward specific objectives. They are like a pilot flying without compass, radar, or landmarks. Result: wasted time and effort.

But that's not very common, is it? Nearly everyone has goals. Most people have in the back of their minds a pretty good idea of what they want to accomplish. Why even mention anything so elementary?

Because a "pretty good idea" isn't good enough and because "in the back of their minds" isn't where those goals should be—they should be on paper.

When you reduce your goals to writing you crystallize your thoughts. Instead of a generality like "financial security," you write down a net worth of a certain amount or a certain level of income; instead of a banal goal like "happiness," you write down the specific things you want that would make you happy, such as a particular kind of work, or achieving a specific objective; instead of an all-encompassing but imprecise goal like "good health" you direct your efforts to specific targets, such as a weight loss of so many pounds, or getting your blood pressure to a certain level, or establishing a certain schedule for exercise.

Do your goal setting in writing. A pencil and a piece of paper are two of the most powerful tools of time management. Incidentally, I recommend making separate lists of lifetime goals and short-range objectives.

You seem to be quite a believer in lists. You recommended earlier making those four procrastination lists, and now you're suggesting a list of long-range goals and a list of short-range goals. Aren't your lists of goals likely to overlap the procrastination lists?

Yes, but if they do, so what? No harm is done. However, as a practical matter, I do think you will find it convenient at some point to merge your procrastination lists into your goals lists.

The next step, of course, is to make sure that those lists aren't made and then filed away and forgotten. They must be kept current, and they should be kept where you will see them at least once a week. Then constantly ask yourself whether or not you are spending enough of your time on the things that really matter—the goal-oriented tasks—as distinguished from the trivia.

Next let's take a look at "wheelspinning."

When people get behind in their work they feel guilty. To assuage those feelings of guilt, our tendency is to get busy and do something—it doesn't seem to matter what, just so there's plenty of action.

Just as a wheelspinning car can carve out a big hole in the mud without moving much, so a wheelspinning person can carve out a big gap in a day without achieving much.

This pitfall is related to the previous one, of course. People who are really goal conscious don't spin their wheels. Their purpose is not to look and feel busy, but to achieve.

Is this what some people refer to as the "activity trap"?

Yes. Whenever you feel pressured by time, don't try to solve your problem by more frantic activity. Pause and calmly survey the situation, so that you can "work smarter, not harder."

Next we come to "fire fighting," which means, of course, living in a state of perpetual crisis. Actual fires often result from procrastination—the faulty wiring that somebody meant to have fixed, the pile of oily rags somebody was going to discard, the additional smoke detector somebody intended to buy, the fire extinguisher somebody forgot to recharge, and so on. The metaphorical fires we fight also often involve procrastination—usually the postponement of planning, so that we are suddenly confronted with a situation we haven't prepared for.

Some crises, of course, cannot be prevented, just as some fires cannot. But most could. The secret is to schedule time for planning on a weekly and daily basis. Think in terms of fire prevention instead of fire fighting.

One helpful technique is to try to schedule your time as much as possible around opportunities rather than problems. It's tempting to put off taking advantage of opportunities, which usually aren't urgent, and to focus entirely on problems, which usually are. But this is a recipe for frustration, failure, and perennial crises. Many of those opportunities you tend to neglect are ways of gaining lead time, thus preventing a crisis farther down the road.

That sounds easy, but the pressures of the day make it hard to put that advice into effect. Any suggestions on how to make it happen?

Yes, follow the suggestion I made earlier. Beginning immediately, make it an ironclad rule to schedule a block of time every day for something that does *not* have to be done that day—but that is important in the long run. (Usually it will turn out to be something relating to one of your long-range goals.) Make it a substantial block of time, perhaps an hour. And guard it jealously: whatever urgent tasks you have to do surely can be accomplished sometime during the remaining twenty-three hours.

This one habit can help you to overcome the most pernicious variety of procrastination, which is the postponing of those important (but not urgent) tasks that would move you toward your major goals.

Next among the cardinal sins is vacillation, the habit of being indecisive.

As mentioned earlier, indecision not only delays resolution of the problem at hand, but it also has a debilitating psychological effect.

Ivan Pavlov, the famous Russian psychologist, once demonstrated how immobilizing the effects of indecision can be. He trained a dog to know he was about to be fed whenever a circle of light was flashed on a screen. Whenever the light was elliptical, no food could be expected.

Then Pavlov gradually changed the shape of the ellipse, making it more nearly circular. At first the dog had no problem; it adjusted to the slight modification. But when the circle became almost, but not quite, circular, the dog became extremely upset, undecided about whether it was looking at a circle or an ellipse, expecting to be fed and not fed at the same time. This indecision created inordinate stress, much more intense than that of normal hunger. Pavlov described the dog's behavior: "It began to squeal in its stand, kept wriggling about . . . and, on being taken into the experimental room, barked violently."[1]

So decisiveness not only gets things done, but reduces stress and makes you feel better, too. In one of Thornton Burgess's classic stories for children, a wise philosopher named the Red Squirrel says:

Though right or wrong, you're bound to find
Relief in making up your mind.

Repeat that little couplet to yourself next time you're writhing in the throes of indecision.

You mention dawdling as another of the cardinal sins.

True. It's often nothing more than a bad habit we drift into because of failure to keep our goals clearly in mind. We fiddle with a task, spending an hour on something that might be done in ten minutes if we shifted into high gear.

Nip this tendency in the bud whenever you notice it. What you're up against, of course, is Parkinson's Law: Work expands to fill the time available. So the solution is to make *less* time available—give yourself a deadline, and perhaps promise yourself some token reward if you meet it. Keep in mind that the tempo at which you work can make a tremendous difference in the amount of time you'll have for other things. You can often more than double your output during a given period by just being aware of tempo, giving yourself that little additional push you need to get on with it, instead of dillydallying.

Just a moment. It appears that you are recommending that people keep their noses to the grindstone all the time, working at maximum capacity throughout the day.

Not at all. I believe in relaxation, in breaks, in moderation, in working at a comfortable pace. But dawdling isn't working, and it isn't really pleasurable or restful or productive. It's a psychological drain, and it's the stuff of which procrastination is made. Work while you work, and rest while you rest; don't try to do both at the same time.

The next of the cardinal sins is the one I call "spraying."

And what does that mean?

The term is borrowed from Sydney J. Harris. In his book *Winners and Losers*,[2] he says, "Winners focus; losers spray."

Just as the gentle rays of the sun, when focused, can burn through steel plate, so moderate skills, when focused on a single task, can accomplish miracles. On the other hand, diversification of effort—spraying—guarantees squandering both skills and time.

Emerson used a tree as an analogy. He said: "As the gardener, by severe pruning, forces the sap of the tree into one or two vigorous limbs, so should you stop off your miscellaneous activity and concentrate your force on one or a few points." One way to accomplish this is to follow the advice of Emerson's famous tenant, Henry David Thoreau: "Simplicity, simplicity, simplicity! I say, let your affairs be as two or three, and not a hundred or a thousand; instead of a million count half a dozen, and keep your accounts on your thumb-nail."

Vince Lombardi was sometimes criticized for using a smaller repertoire of plays than most coaches, but he believed that even when working with top professional athletes it was better to focus on a relatively few plays, and master them completely, rather than to risk the "spraying" effect by having too many options available. "It's difficult to be aggressive when confused," he said.

You've occasionally been amazed at how much you accomplished when an imminent deadline or a crisis forced you to stop "spraying" and to focus all of your energy and attention on a single activity. Force yourself to display that same singleness of purpose whenever you undertake *any* task, and you'll amaze yourself every day!

Besides avoiding the tendency to "spray" you must also beware of the tendency to switch.

What do you mean by that?

Aside from concentration, you must also develop staying power. Even if you concentrate, if you don't do it long enough—if you continually switch from one thing to another—you will be ineffective. You must develop what has been called the "compulsion to closure."[3]

But sometimes it makes sense to switch. Occasionally when you're working on something and reach a dead end you realize that putting it aside for a while to work on something else might restore your perspective. You don't object to that, do you?

Of course not. What I'm talking about is the habit of getting something partly done, and then getting sidetracked and drifting to something else, like a butterfly flitting from one flower to another.

Don't be too easy-going with yourself when you assume that putting the thing aside for a while may be useful. Maybe it will; but maybe a little stick-to-it-iveness would be even more useful.

Persistence is what we're talking about. Calvin Coolidge is not one of our more frequently quoted presidents, but he made one observation that I think is worth committing to memory (as a matter of fact, I have it on a plaque in my study). He said:

> Nothing in the world can take the place of persistence. Talent will not; nothing is more common than unsuccessful men with talent. Genius will not; unrewarded genius is almost a proverb. Education alone will not; the world is full of educated derelicts. Persistence and determination alone are omnipotent.[4]

Let's persistently proceed with your list. The next pitfall you mentioned was "acquiescing." What do you mean by that?

Too often the source of our time shortage is simply that we haven't learned to use that simple little two-letter word "No." We see the pattern in volunteer organizations, at work, in the home; someone twists our arm a bit and asks us to do something we really don't want to do, but rather than asserting our right to set our own priorities we accept the assignment. Then we kick ourselves later, but we're stuck.

That sounds rather coldhearted. The person who asks you wouldn't be seeking your help if it weren't needed. As a loyal member, employee, friend, spouse, parent, or whatever, shouldn't you cheerfully demonstrate your willingness to cooperate?

Yes—up to a point. We all want to contribute to society and to our organizations and our families; most of us are happy to do our fair share. But when, because of timidity or misplaced altruism, we accept responsibilities that are too burdensome, we are being unfair to our family, our associates, our organization, and ourselves. Some groups and some people are insensitive and insatiable in their demands. To overcommit your time in such circumstances should be thought of as weakness, not willingness.

A certain amount of give and take is implicit in any relationship, and we all frequently will yield to the wishes of a friend or loved one. But when that other person begins to push too hard, demanding so much of you that your own needs and interests are trampled, it's time for a forthright expression of your feelings. You needn't be antagonistic— don't accuse the other person of taking advantage of you— just talk about your own feelings: "I feel that what you've asked me to do will take time that I had planned to devote to certain other things that are important to me, so I'm going to have to say 'No.'" How much better it is to bring the matter out into the open this way, instead of resentfully accepting the assignment and then wondering why you did!

The ninth item on your list was "rehashing." What is rehashing, and why should it be avoided?

I use that term to describe the tendency to dwell in the past, reliving experiences that are over and done with, rethinking decisions that have already been acted on, wasting time and energy in either reminiscence or regret.

Everyone does a certain amount of this, of course, but some people become virtual captives of the past. Some continually bemoan the mistakes or misfortunes of days gone by, living lives of frustration and resentment; others focus on past victories and achievements, replaying the mental tapes of yesterday's applause. In either case, today's opportunities and challenges are ignored. The results are passivity, procrastination, and inaction. One of the greatest mistakes we can make is to concern ourselves too much with what was and what might have been, instead of what is and what can be.

Banish the past. Put those mental tapes away until you're in your nineties, when there'll be time enough for reminiscence. Meanwhile, you have a future to be concerned about, and that future will be shaped for better or worse by what you do—or fail to do—today.

Make today count!

That sporty little sermon leaves just one remaining item on your list of the Terrible Ten: "perfecting." How does it relate to management of time?

Perfectionism causes procrastination in two separate ways. One way, which we discussed in connection with fear of failure, results in immobility. Many people think that anything short of perfection is failure. Not wanting to fail, they avoid it in the only way possible under that definition: they refuse to try. They may refuse outright, or to deceive themselves or others they may hide their refusal behind the mask of procrastination.

So one manifestation of perfectionism is simply not trying. The other, which concerns time management, is exactly the opposite. The person *does* undertake the task, but spends so much time perfecting every espect of it that there isn't time left for other activities that are equally (or more) desirable.

You seem to be advocating that people be satisfied with something short of their very best. Those extra efforts that may take additional time sometimes make a big difference. They may seem like trifles, but as Michelangelo said, "Trifles make perfection, and perfection is no trifle." You appear to be willing to settle for mediocrity.

Not at all. Perfection, fortunately, is not the only alternative to mediocrity. A more sensible alternative is excellence. Striving for excellence is stimulating and rewarding; striving for perfection—in practically anything—is both neurotic and futile.

Oh, I suppose if you were Michelangelo, painting the ceiling of the Sistine Chapel, we might make an exception—although even there I think there comes a time when you must say, "I could add another angel here, and I could touch up Jeremiah's beard a bit, and I could remove Adam's belly button to avoid some awkward speculation about how it got there, but it just isn't worth it. That's good enough!" (In addition to that quotation about perfection, I believe Michelangelo is also credited with saying, "The secret of art is knowing when to stop.")

Few houses are so clean that they couldn't be a little cleaner, few letters so well worded that they couldn't be refined a bit, few gardens so immaculate that they contain not a single weed. But if you squander your limited supply of time striving for perfection in those things, some other activity must suffer. Ask yourself what other things you might accomplish with that same time, and ask whether you really want to pay the price.

Author Gail Sheehy put it this way: "Would that there were an award for people who come to understand the concept of enough. Good enough. Successful enough. Thin enough. Rich enough. Socially responsible enough. When you have self-respect, you have enough; and when you have enough, you have self-respect."[5]

To add anything to that would be . . . well, more than enough!

Taking the Tenth Step

Give yourself the following quiz:

	YES	NO
1. Do I have in writing *a list of my life-time goals*?	☐	☐
2. Do I have a list of short-range (six-month) goals?	☐	☐
3. Do I keep those lists where I will see them often, so they will influence my daily and weekly planning?	☐	☐
4. Do I try to plan as much as possible in terms of importance rather than urgency?	☐	☐
5. When a flap occurs, do I force myself to pause and map out the best course of action, instead of just getting busy and spinning my wheels? In other words, do I really try to "work smarter rather than harder"?	☐	☐
6. Do I force myself to make decisions promptly, and then concentrate on carrying them out, instead of constantly fretting about whether I made the best decision?	☐	☐
7. Do I focus as intently as possible on one thing at a time, stubbornly resisting thoughts or actions extraneous to the matter at hand?	☐	☐
8. Once I begin something, do I always strive for closure?	☐	☐
9. Do I make ample use of the word no to avoid taking on responsibilities that should belong to someone else?	☐	☐

	YES	NO

10. *Do I try to live in the present, directing my thoughts away from what I should have done "then" and toward what I should do "now"?* ☐ ☐

11. *When working on a task am I always alert for the point of diminishing returns, where additional effort and time would cross over the line between striving for excellence and striving for perfection?* ☐ ☐

12. *If I answered* no *to any of the foregoing questions, am I going to take appropriate corrective action—*now? ☐

Use Visible Reminders

Procrastination is such an insidious habit that it creeps up on us unaware. Is there any way a person can be assured of not forgetting the principles we've been discussing?

Many people find it helpful to put reminders where they will see them occasionally during the day. At home you can stick them on your bathroom mirror, on the television set, on the dashboard of your car, in your handbag, in your wallet. At work you might put them on your phone, on your desk pad, on your calendar, in the john, on the wall, on your typewriter, on a paperweight, and so on.

165

Dr. Janette Rainwater, a clinical psychologist, describes a typical application of this technique:

> One of my people discovered that she went to the refrigerator every time she started thinking about all the great things she could have done with her life and hadn't. As a result of this realization, she painted a sign and hung it on the refrigerator: "This is the door to your refrigerator, not the door to success." The second time she caught herself about to quiet her frustrations with food, she slammed the refrigerator door shut, got in her car, drove to the local college and enrolled for the next quarter.[1]

No matter how well we know something, seeing it repeatedly in writing intensifies its impact. Golfer Johnny Miller, for example, carries around an old brown envelope on which he writes little reminders to himself—"Take the club back slowly," "Make sure you are comfortable before starting the swing," etc. He says, "I believe the brain is a computer. If you keep feeding things into it, it remembers and transfers them to the body. That's why all the sayings are positive. Actually, they're commands."

Some people prefer to select a single phrase as their permanent motto. I have one friend who has had *When are you going to do it?* pasted inside his attaché case for as long as I've known him. Others prefer to select a "Thought for the Week," or even a "Thought for the Day."

Others like to display a quotation from some well-known author, such as Shakespeare.

Shakespeare? Was he an expert on procrastination?

He certainly was. Anyone who can grind out more than a million imperishable words, while at the same time working as an actor and businessman, has mastered the art of getting on with the task at hand. As for his writing, I don't know that he ever used the word "procrastination," but as Goethe said, "Whatever can be known of the human heart may be found in Shakespeare's plays," and one of the foibles of the human heart has always been the tendency to temporize.

Shakespeare's works abound with admonitions to avoid procrastination. "If it were done when 'tis done, then 'twere well it were done quickly," says Macbeth. "Defer no time, delays have dangerous ends," says Reignier in *King Henry VI*. "There is a tide in the affairs of men which taken at the flood leads on to fortune; omitted, all the voyage of their life is bound in shallows and in miseries," says Brutus in *Julius Caesar*. "We must take the current when it serves, or lose our ventures."

Though he earned his living with words, Shakespeare had contempt for those who use words as a substitute for deeds. "Action is eloquence," said this most eloquent of men, and he urged that we "suit the action to the word." He reminded us that "Thoughts are but dreams till their effects be tried," and said, "Let's take the instant by the forward top, for we are old, and on our quickest decrees, the inaudible and noiseless foot of time steals, ere we can effect them."

Always mindful of that "inaudible and noiseless foot of time," he reminds us again and again that "The time of life is short; to spend that shortness basely were too long." His sonnets are replete with references to Time's tyranny, Time's fell hand, Time's thievish progress to eternity, devouring Time, sluttish Time, and the chronicle of wasted time. And, since "nothing 'gainst Time's scythe can make defence," he warned that "we must not stint our necessary actions." If we do, we "play the fools with the time; and the spirits of the wise sit in the clouds and mock us."

And if you habitually put your trust in what you are going to do tomorrow, remember that "Tomorrow and tomorrow and tomorrow creeps in this petty pace from day to day, to the last syllable of recorded time. . . ." I don't think procrastination is what Shakespeare had in mind when he had Macbeth utter that memorable line, but I don't believe he would mind our disregarding the context if it serves a useful purpose. Surely "petty pace" does describe the rate at which we move toward our goals if we always think in terms of acting tomorrow!

You appear to have a very high regard for Shakespeare as a proponent of getting things done promptly.

I do indeed. However, before we nominate him for the Anti-Procrastination Hall of Fame, it would be only fair to point out that we know he himself was guilty of at least one notable instance of procrastination during his lifetime: he didn't get around to marrying the mother of his children until six months before the birth of their first child—which just goes to show that even the wisest among us sometimes have a tendency to "stint our necessary actions."

We seem to be digressing. To get back to mottoes and slogans, are there any that you particularly recommend?

The most succinct all-purpose reminder is, simply, *DO IT NOW!* Seeing those three little words many times a day can pound a trenchant message into your brain. W. Clement Stone, president of the Combined Group of Companies and publisher of *Success*, recommends that you not only put those words where you will see them frequently, but that you repeat them aloud fifty times each morning and fifty times each evening for a week or so to imprint them indelibly on your subconscious. (This technique of endowing words with power by repeating them aloud is well recognized in religion; every church uses verbal repetition in its rituals. Perhaps you can devise some rituals of your own to help strengthen your resolve.)

Following are some other mottoes, many of which I have picked up from participants in my time management and anti-procrastination seminars. (Keep in mind, these are listed because they may help you avoid procrastination, not because they are especially clever or amusing. If it's smart-ass humor you're looking for, you can find that on the nearest bumper sticker.)

Tomorrow is never

◆

Make today count

◆

Procrastination prevents success

◆

Doing beats stewing

◆

In just two days, tomorrow will be yesterday

◆

Time is money

◆

Do it anyway!

◆

Get the now habit

◆

People don't fail because they intend to fail;
they fail because they fail to do what they intend to do

◆

Get a round tuit

◆

Be a doer, not a dawdler

◆

Why wait?

◆

Don't delay—do it today

◆

Have a happy tomorrow:
Do today's work today

◆

Prō·crăs´·tĭ·nā´·shŭn: a dream deferred

◆

If not today—WHEN?

◆

Today: Use it or lose it

◆

Use this day well

◆

Life is leaking through your fingers

◆

Do it before sundown

◆

You don't find time—you make it!

◆

Just do it!

◆

"Mean to" don't pick no cotton

◆

Make it happen

◆

Only turkeys procrastinate

◆

Yesterday is a cancelled check: forget it
Tomorrow is a promissory note: don't count on it
Today is ready cash: use it!

◆

Lead time: The gift that only I can give myself

◆

Due tomorrow? Do today!

◆

Trying to do something and failing
Is better than trying to do nothing and succeeding

◆

Well begun is half done

◆

Get off your duff

◆

If it's worth doing, it's worth doing now

◆

If it's to be, it's up to me

◆

Move ahead or move aside

◆

Winners don't wait

◆

Choose this day to use this day

◆

Do it or ditch it

◆

There's a time to work
and a time to play . . .
It's time to work

◆

If you have to do it—do it now!

◆

Procrastination is the thief of time

◆

Tomorrow is too late

◆

Do the worst first

◆

When tomorrow comes, what am I going to wish I had
done today?

◆

Doing gets it done

◆

A journey of a thousand miles begins with a single step:
take it!

Some people prefer to use foreign phrases, such as
tempus fugit or *carpe diem*, because they seem more esoteric
—or because the phrases seem more private. (I recall that
my father, who as a young man had learned Hawaiian, used
to write reminders to himself in that language to insure
privacy. Needless to say, it worked.)

Still others like to use initials as reminders. One friend of mine has the letters DIND emblazoned on his desk lamp; if pressed, he will admit that they stand for Do It Now, Dummy! Another executive I know has the letters QFA elegantly engraved on a plaque on his wall. The meaning, politely translated, is Quit Foolin' Around.

Taking the Eleventh Step

From the maxims in the preceding chapter, select the one that you think would be most likely to push you into action if you saw it repeatedly. Or, if you prefer, make up your own—some little nugget of advice that you know, if followed, could change your life. Then inscribe it on your bathroom mirror, or tape it in your wallet, or embroider it on your favorite pillow, or have it translated into Latin and incorporate it into your family coat of arms.* Anything to make sure that you'll notice it many times a day. And every time you see it, remember that it's not a decoration, but a call to action, so do what it says.

Now!

---

* The late George Meany, president of the AFL-CIO, found it helpful to have on his wall the inscription *"Illegitimi Non Carborundum"*— which translates as "Don't Let the Bastards Wear You Down."

Step
12

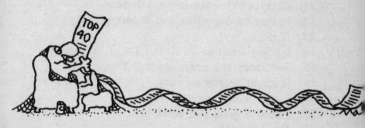

Learn to Deal with
the Top Forty Cop-outs

The recording companies periodically put out a list of the Top Forty hits. If you were to make a list of the top forty excuses for procrastination, what would it look like?

I would guess that the forty most commonly used reasons are:

1. It's unpleasant.
2. It's not due yet.
3. I work better under pressure.
4. Maybe it will take care of itself if I just don't do anything.

5. It's too early in the day.
6. It's too late in the day.
7. I don't have my papers with me.
8. It's difficult.
9. I don't feel like doing it now.
10. I have a headache.
11. Delay won't make much difference.
12. It may be important, but it isn't urgent.
13. It might hurt.
14. I really mean to do it, but I keep forgetting.
15. Somebody else might do it if I wait.
16. It might be embarrassing.
17. I don't know where to begin.
18. I need a good stiff drink first.
19. I'm too tired.
20. I'm too busy right now.
21. It's a boring job.
22. It might not work.
23. I've got to tidy up first.
24. I need to sleep on it.
25. We can get by a little longer as is.
26. I don't really know how to do it.
27. There's a good TV program on.
28. As soon as I start, somebody will probably interrupt.
29. It needs further study.
30. My horoscope indicates this is the wrong time.
31. Nobody is nagging me about it yet.
32. If I do it now, they'll just give me something else to do.
33. The weather's lousy.
34. It's too nice a day to spend doing that.
35. Before I start, I think I'll take a break.
36. I'll do it as soon as I finish some preliminary tasks.
37. My biorhythms are out of sync.

38. The sooner I fall behind, the more time I'll have to get caught up.
39. I'll wait until the first of the year and make a New Year's resolution.
40. It's too late now, anyway.

That's a pretty impressive list. But most of those reasons could be valid in many cases, couldn't they?

Of course. That's the trouble with procrastination. It's so easy to come up with a legitimate excuse and use it where it really shouldn't apply. To counter this, you must develop an automatic self-dialogue mechanism that will be triggered whenever you are tempted to use one of those phrases. You must ask yourself constantly, "Am I analyzing or rationalizing?"

Let's take these Top Forty reasons one by one, and examine the kinds of arguments you should consider when you're tempted to wander down the Primrose Path of Procrastination:

1. It's unpleasant.

No doubt it is. But is it going to become less unpleasant as time goes on? Quite the contrary: most things get worse when you put them off, and in the meantime you have to put up with a nagging conscience. Honestly now, wouldn't you feel better if you traded a little discomfort today for the satisfaction of getting that task done, once and for all?

Happiness is crossing off a nasty item on your To Do list.

2. It's not due yet.

Right! So now you have an opportunity instead of a problem. An opportunity to gain some lead time, to do the job the way it ought to be done, to be in control and to work at your own pace instead of being a slave to a clock or a calendar. And for what it's worth, you have a chance to score some points with people you work with—your boss, your associates, your subordinates, your customers, your family—who will be impressed with your determination to tackle an unpleasant job and get it over with promptly (which, incidentally, may encourage them to do likewise). More important, you have a chance to score some points with yourself, to build self-esteem by proving to yourself that you're a self-starter.

So what are you waiting for?

3. I work better under pressure.

This ploy is one of the most insidious of all the arguments for procrastination. It does, of course, contain an element of truth: most of us, when the pressure is on, do force ourselves to concentrate, to block out extraneous diversions, to "grasp the nettle," and to do what needs to be done. But a little self-discipline can create just as much pressure while protecting the cushion of time that can be so valuable if something unexpected occurs, or if the job simply takes longer than anticipated.

So *create* some pressure. Give yourself a deadline, and be tough about meeting it. Take all the legitimate shortcuts that you would take if you were forced to do the job at the last minute. Just because you have the luxury of a little breathing space doesn't mean that you have to dawdle!

4. Maybe the task will take care of itself if I just ignore it long enough.

Fat chance! Oh, it happens sometimes, I know. You ignore the thump under the hood of your car, and it mysteriously stops, or you postpone the visit to the doctor and the pains in your chest go away. Still, you are left wondering whether you did the right thing. You must weigh the pros and cons, and recognize that although the problem might go away, it might not—and you must consider the possible consequences.

We tend not to do this. We tell ourselves that the matter will take care of itself when objective analysis would lead us to the opposite conclusion. For example, I have never known a leaky faucet to repair itself, or a stack of paperwork to sort itself out, or a basement to clean itself up, or an apology to make itself spontaneously. Yet we act as if we half-expect these miracles to happen!

5. *It's too early in the day.*

Some salespeople make frequent use of this one, believing that it's better not to make calls before prospects have a chance to handle the mail and get their day started. The successful ones, however, recognize this rationalization for what it is: an excuse for indolence. Waiting for the "perfect" time means squandering a lot of "pretty good" time, which is a luxury none of us can afford. Since the early bird catches the worm, it's a good idea to begin your day as soon as you can—unless, of course, you happen to be a worm.

6. *It's too late in the day.*

Another handy excuse for those who are looking for reasons not to do what they should. To take salespeople again as an example, it's so tempting to assume that a call on a customer at 4:30 P.M. will be wasted, because the customer is getting ready to leave the office. But successful salespeople know that one of the secrets of success is the extra business they can get by making just one more call every day before quitting, rather than conning themselves into calling only at the "optimum" time. It's the same in any field: *no one has enough time to be able to use only the ideal moments*. The remnants of time must be used because they too are precious.

7. *I don't have my papers with me* (or my tools, or my glasses, or my briefcase, or whatever).

Sometimes this is because of a subconscious decision *not* to have the necessary items with you in order to give yourself an excuse for inaction. Ask yourself *why* you don't have what you need and what you are going to do to avoid getting caught again without the required materials. Then, to teach yourself that such avoidance techniques simply won't work, force yourself to do the best you can right now anyway!

8. *It's difficult.*

If you let yourself get away with this one, you're really in trouble. So it's difficult; so what? You've done lots of difficult things before, haven't you? And will it become any less difficult as a result of delay? The answers to these questions are obvious; the trouble is that the questions don't get asked.

Never let the difficulty of a task stand as an adequate reason for not acting; force yourself to identify precisely what is to be gained in the long run by delay. In most cases you'll find you can't.

The harder something is, the greater the challenge and the sweeter the fruits of accomplishment. There's genuine satisfaction in victory over hardship—especially if you were on the attack, if you moved in and handled the problem resolutely instead of waiting until circumstances forced you to act.

9. *I don't feel like doing it now.*

Good. That gives you a wonderful opportunity to prove to yourself that you are not a captive of your moods. Select a starting point, take a deep breath, and begin. It's amazing how quickly a negative mood can evaporate when you take resolute action. Think of your lackadaisical mood not as a reason for delay but as a byproduct of inactivity. So the antidote for such a mood is—you guessed it—activity!

10. *I have a headache.*

Like many other reasons, this may be a legitimate reason for delay or it may not. Instead of just putting the desired task aside, try to determine the reason for the headache. If it is accompanied by other symptoms, such as impaired vision, nausea, fever, dizzy spells, swelling ankles, or a pounding heart, by all means consult your physician. A headache isn't always "just in your head,"—it can be a symptom of a number of physical ailments. Or it may result from some external factor, such as bad lighting, noise, inadequate ventilation, poor posture, or an out-of-date eyeglass prescription, in which case the solution is self-evident. Don't put off doing something about it.

But if it seems to be caused by stress that is related to a particular activity—for example, if you get a headache every time you get ready to begin a certain task your boss has asked you to do—try to pinpoint the real cause of that stress. Is it because you have inadequate tools? Is it because you lack certain information? Is it a result of a double bind—a damned-if-you-do, damned-if-you-don't situation? Is it because you feel great pressure to perform, but are unsure precisely what is expected? Is it because the task offends your sense of values? Is it because you consider it a waste of your time?

Once you have determined why this particular task gives you a headache, face up to the problem rather than just putting it on the back burner, where it will continue to simmer and produce stress. If it involves your boss, spouse, or an associate, confront him or her and try to work out a solution. Even if you don't resolve the problem, you can often reduce tension by just getting it out into the open.

Don't forget, though, that in many cases the best way to deal with a stress headache is just to tackle the job that's worrying you instead of putting it off any longer. Quite often that turns out to be the miracle cure!

11. Delay won't make much difference.

This is perhaps the most common rationalization of all—and the most erroneous.

Delay *does* made a difference, nearly always. It diminishes the chance that the task will ever get done; it increases the likelihood that it will be done haphazardly; it robs you of the confidence that comes from knowing that you are completely in control; and it reinforces a bad habit that is sure to cause you trouble in connection with other matters.

On the other hand, there are times when delay *is* justified. Maybe the timing is bad, maybe more information is needed, maybe more help will be available at a later time, maybe there is something of higher priority that should be done first. If so, base the postponement on a cool, hard-headed decision that delay would have specific advantages—not on the specious argument that it "doesn't make any difference."

12. It may be important, but it isn't urgent.

The greatest mistake you can make is to let your actions be determined solely by urgency, rather than importance; that, in a nutshell, is the pitfall of the perennial procrastinator.

Whenever you have a choice to make between two actions, ask not which is the more insistent, or the more immediate, or the more visible; ask which really matters more in the long run.

Operating out of urgency is exemplified by the Squeaking Wheel method of setting priorities. The squeaking wheel on the wagon demands attention, and perhaps should get it—but it might be wiser to turn attention first to another wheel that is silently carrying its burden, but is about to fall apart.

Over and over again, ask yourself, "Does this really matter in the long run, or doesn't it?" Then act accordingly.

13. It might hurt.

It would be interesting to know how many miles of root canal work have been performed because people postponed getting small cavities filled on the grounds that "it might hurt."

Think about that.

14. I really mean to do it, but I keep forgetting.

This means one of two things: either you forget because deep down you don't really want to do the thing (debtors have worse memories than creditors, as Ben Franklin observed), or you forget because you don't have a system to help you remember.

If it's the former, some soul-searching is in order. Quit kidding yourself about "forgetting," and try to unearth the real reason for your convenient memory lapse. Is it fear of failure? Fear of success? Conflicting priorities? Resentment? Jealousy? Laziness? Embarrassment? Lack of skill? Self-defeating habits? Low self-esteem? If it's any of these, perhaps some of the points discussed elsewhere in this book will be of help. On the other hand—let's face it—self-help may not be the solution. It works for many, but sometimes there's no substitute for counseling. Chronic procrastination can be symptomatic of deep-seated emotional problems, and do-it-yourself psychiatry is by no means as successful as do-it-yourself carpentry.

If, however, your forgetfulness is simply what it appears to be, it shouldn't be all that hard to rectify. A note to yourself, a desk calendar entry, a tickler file, a sign on the wall, a wristwatch alarm, the old-fashioned string around the finger, a rubber band on the wrist, a spouse or associate who will agree to nag you—there are innumerable devices and techniques for helping you to remember, if that's actually your problem. Give them a try.

15. If I put it off, somebody else might do it.

That may get the job done, but it won't do much for your reputation among your associates, assuming that you are the logical person to have done the task. It won't do much for your self-esteem, either, knowing that some poor fall guy is stuck with doing your work. George Washington spoke of "that little spark of celestial fire, conscience." Your spark hasn't gone out, has it?

16. It might be embarrassing.

What you should really be embarrassed about is permitting yourself to postpone on such flimsy grounds an action you know you should take. Mentally rehearse doing the thing, and mentally rehearse how you will respond if the worst imaginable situation develops, and you'll soon find yourself making plans and backup plans, and thinking constructively about the task, instead of indulging in agonizing (and as yet undeserved) self-pity.

Some of the suggestions in Chapters 2, 3, and 6 also might help.

17. I don't know where to begin: the job is overwhelming.

Time to use the Salami Technique that we discussed in Chapter 2. Break the job down—on paper—into as many tiny steps as you can.

As your grandmother probably taught you,

> *Life by the yard is apt to be hard;*
> *Life by the inch is more of a cinch.*

18. I need a good stiff drink first.

Those are ominous words; they imply that you're using liquor as a crutch to get you through difficult situations, and when that happens you're on a collision course with disaster. If you can't force yourself to postpone that drink until you've accomplished the task, the procrastination you should be worrying about is the phone call to Alcoholics Anonymous that you've been putting off. You'll find AA listed in the white pages of your phone book.

19. I'm too tired.

Remember the warning of William James about too readily accepting this excuse for inaction. Learn to look for the "second wind" that comes quite often if you just hang in there for a few minutes longer. Don't call it quits every time you run into that "first layer of fatigue."

20. I'm too busy right now.

A fine, universal, irrefutable, all-purpose rationalization for the would-be procrastinator. And even if it isn't technically true at the moment, you can quickly make it true by finding something to get busy on, however trivial. It's self-satisfying, too, because you can always fool yourself into thinking you are overworked.

But wait a minute. Before letting yourself off the hook so easily, ask yourself about the comparative importance and urgency of the task you're putting off and the one you're doing instead. Do you really have your priorities straight? If so, fine: put it off with a clear conscience. You aren't procrastinating, you are following priorities. However, if the task you're giving priority to is more fun but less rewarding in the long run, you know what to do, and I trust you'll do it.

21. It's a boring job.

Every job, every accomplishment, has its monotonous aspects. Playing scales on the piano, for example, is tedium itself; but it builds the dexterity that later will permit the pianist to pour out his soul through the keyboard. Nothing could be more boring to a football player than calisthenics and sprints, but a team that omitted this boring routine from its preseason training would be denying itself the exhilaration of future victory.

There's always a trade-off. The trick is to keep your mind on what you'll get in return for what you give—even if it's just the satisfaction of seeing the astonished look on your boss's face when you finish a distasteful task ahead of schedule.

22. It might not work.

There's one way to find out, isn't there?

23. I've got to tidy up first.

Like so many other excuses, this one may or may not be valid. If "tidy up" means to gather a bunch of scattered papers and put them out of your way, so you can concentrate on the task at hand, by all means do so. But if it means going through a stack of papers one by one and getting them all sorted into a new pattern, followed by some filing, followed by a bit of dusting and polishing, ask yourself if this isn't a diversionary routine. You seem to have this compulsion to sort, file, dust, and polish. Fine: why not use that compulsion, then, as a reinforcer? Why not promise yourself that you'll do those things as soon as you complete the less enjoyable task that you know in your heart has a greater payoff?

24. I need to sleep on it.

Some matters need to incubate for a while, to be sure. But most don't. Too often when you sleep on something, it winds up being squashed.

25. We can get by a little longer as is.

Perhaps. But if you're going to have to take the plunge eventually—why not now? Why not avert a crisis by acting before you are compelled to? Why not act, instead of reacting? Why not play the game of life on the offense, instead of the defense?

Remember: it is better to deal with difficulty today than disaster tomorrow.

26. I don't really know how to do it.

If you lack knowledge or skills that are needed to do a task, obviously you shouldn't blame yourself for not doing it. But you *should* blame yourself if you don't take the steps to gain that knowledge or those skills—or to arrange to have the job done by someone who does have them. In any event, the ball is in your court. If you can't do the job, give it to someone else, but do *something*—don't just procrastinate.

27. *There's a good TV program on.*

Two decades ago, FCC Chairman Newton Minow referred to television as a "vast wasteland." The phrase still applies, and it conjures up in my mind's eye a landscape littered with countless ruins of unfulfilled plans, aborted ventures, unrealized dreams—not just on the part of the producers, but also of the viewers, who try to select the least tedious of several mediocre shows instead of turning the set off and doing something. If the activity you are postponing really ranks below the typical situation comedy or quiz show in priority, then it's not worth doing at all, so forget it. But give some thought to whether you ought to be striving for some more challenging goals.

28. *As soon as I start, somebody will probably interrupt.*

If the hustle and bustle around you is creating a mental block, do something about your environment. Seclude yourself, if you can. Close the door and resolve not to open it until the task is done. At a minimum, tell the people around you that you need some time to concentrate (and let them know what the task is that you're working on, so you have the added prod of having made a commitment to do it). Explain that you would like to be incommunicado until you finish. It won't always work, but you'll be surprised how often it will. People tend to respect the privacy of someone who seems determined to concentrate on a task until it's done.

29. *It needs further study.*

Everything does. Meanwhile, go ahead on the basis of what you know, if you have a pretty good hunch as to what that further study is likely to confirm. Remember the words of the ancient maxim: "He who considers too much will perform little."

30. My horoscope indicates this is the wrong time.

Far be it from me to want to come between you and your astrologer. And yet . . . well, let's put it this way: I'm told that astrologers, like surgeons, sometimes disagree. Before you ever postpone anything on purely astrological grounds, may I suggest that you at least consider getting a second opinion?

31. Nobody is nagging me about it yet.

To say this is to admit that you have abdicated your decision-making power to others. If somebody is going to be "on your case," that somebody should be you.

Many years ago, David Riesman[1] coined the terms "other-directed" and "inner-directed" to distinguish between people who act primarily out of concern for what others think and say and those who act because of their own convictions and perceptions.

Inner-directed is the way to go.

32. If I do it now they'll just give me something else to do.

People usually don't express this attitude quite so openly, but the rationale is not all that uncommon.

If you find yourself feeling this way it's time to do some soul-searching, because you are in a situation that will never provide you any real satisfaction. What you are saying is that you don't care about the aims or achievements of the institution you are working for, and you have no desire to pull your weight within the organization. You have, in short, reached the dead end of other-directedness.

You have two constructive options: you can overhaul your attitude, and try to act on the basis of what needs to be done, instead of on what "they" might tell you to do, or you can leave the organization and try to connect with one whose goals matter to you.

The third choice, which is to accept the status quo and continue to make a minimal contribution, is the cowardly way out, although it's the way many people choose. I feel sorry for them, because it isn't very rewarding to be, in effect, a living puppet—and a reluctant one at that.

33. *The weather's lousy.*

The term *weather permitting* is properly applied to announcements of parades and outdoor weddings, but most of life's activities must go on, weather or not. The jogger who does his thing only when the temperature is perfect and the skies are blue will never develop much stamina, physically or mentally. Growth comes from surmounting circumstances, not from yielding to them.

34. *It's too nice a day to spend doing that.*

Some people can find good weather or bad weather equally convenient as an excuse for not doing what they should be doing. Amazing, isn't it?

And yet—let's face it—there are times when one should close up shop and go fishing, if one has that option. As the Bible says, there is a time to weep and a time to laugh, a time to mourn and a time to dance . . . and, presumably, a time to punch a typewriter and a time to go fishing. The problem is, how can you be sure which time it is?

I think your best bet is to ask yourself how you will feel when it's over. Suppose, for example, you're debating whether to paint the porch Saturday afternoon or whether to take the afternoon off and fly a kite with your kid. How are you likely to feel when you get back from kite-flying? If you'll consider it time well-spent, then that's what it will have been. You didn't procrastinate on painting the porch— you simply did a higher priority activity. To have done otherwise would have been to procrastinate on spending some time with your child!

On the other hand, if you would feel guilty and resentful while flying that kite, and if you would return with regrets that you didn't stay and paint the porch, then perhaps the kite-flying at that particular time would be a mistake. So let your anticipated hindsight determine your course of action. Ask yourself how you're going to feel about the decision the next day, when you will be more objective.

(My own feeling, incidentally, is that most of us give such things as kite-flying a much lower priority than they really deserve.)

35. Before starting I think I'll take a break.

(This ploy has many variations—before starting I'm going to have a cigarette, or a snack, or a Coke, or I'm going to read the newspaper.)

This is usually a mistake. Instead of putting off the unpleasant task until after you have done something pleasant, reverse the procedure and use the pleasurable activity as a reward for having begun what you are tempted to postpone. Say to yourself, "Yes, I'm due for a break, but before I begin it I'm going to make at least a start on that unpleasant task." Make that preliminary phone call, or draft the outline, or get out the file and put it where you can't ignore it when you come back—anything to give you a bit of momentum, so that when you return you can land running. (We are assuming here, of course, that the task is a large one. If it's small, then by all means make the break contingent upon finishing it, not just getting started.)

The thing to keep in mind is that to be psychologically effective, reinforcement must come after, not before, the desired behavior.

36. I'll do it as soon as I take care of some preliminary tasks.

Here you are being a little more cunning than in the previous case. Instead of just delaying in order to relax or goof off, you are getting started on a related task, which makes the delay seem justified.

And indeed it may be. Before sawing wood, there's nothing wrong with sharpening your saw if it really needs it. The trouble is that so often these preliminary chores turn out to be *substitute* chores. You decide to sharpen your saw, but you find your file is gummed up. After you clean it, you notice that the workbench vise is wobbly, so you fix that. When you finally get the saw sharpened, you decide that while you're at it you might as well sharpen the other saw, which, incidentally, has a loose handle that needs to be fixed. By now you've forgotten what it was you started out to do, so you spend the next hour reorganizing your tools.

If a preliminary task must be done, do it; but remember that these tasks have a tendency to become red herrings. Keep your mind on the ultimate objective.

37. My biorhythms are out of sync.

The biorhythm fad is harmless enough as a parlor game, but when it becomes an excuse for postponing something you know you should do, it's time to put your biorhythm charts the same place you put your old fortune cookie slips. Your time and your life are too precious to entrust to the vagaries of a silicon soothsayer. As Shakespeare might have said,

> *Men at some times are masters of their fate:*
> *The fault, dear Brutus, is not in our biorhythms,*
> *But in ourselves, that we are underlings.*

38. *The sooner I get behind, the more time I'll have in which to get caught up.*

I've run into this delightful bit of sophistry several times in my time management and anti-procrastination seminars, and I'm still not sure that it's just a put-on. It bears out my contention that experienced procrastinators develop a creative logic all their own.

39. *I'll wait until the first of the year and make a New Year's resolution.*

Or, I'll begin my diet next Monday.

Or, I'll begin practicing good study habits as soon as I get into college.

Or, I'll start exercising regularly as soon as I retire.

This practice of postponing the establishment of a new habit until some date in the future seldom works. It is predicated on the assumption that you are going to have more willpower then than you have now, but you won't. Be honest with yourself: what's the advantage of striking when the iron's cold?

40. *It's too late now, anyway.*

This one is irrefutable. No use closing the barn door after the horse gets out, is there?

But why did the horse get out? Because you were willing to accept one of the 39 other cop-outs as a valid reason for not closing the door when you should have, that's why.

How about it—do you have any barn doors that need closing right now?

A Final Word

By now I consider you a kindred spirit. You share my fascination with this exasperating quirk of human nature called procrastination, or you wouldn't have picked up this book, and you share my conviction that it can be overcome, or you wouldn't have troubled to read to the end.

I wish you success in your efforts. Be assured that you will be rewarded with a new sense of mastery over events and over yourself, and that you will find you are moving ever closer to the heights of self-realization that you hope to reach.

Now, a request: I'm convinced that there is much more to be learned about overcoming procrastination, and I think you can help. Every human being grapples with this tendency every day, and I suspect that additional insights on the sub-ject are not as likely to come from the behavioral scientists as from the non-professionals—from the guy who figures out how to stop postponing that salary confrontation with his boss, or from the woman who figures out a way to make her-self schedule that dental checkup before a toothache per-suades her to, or from the student who comes up with a method for getting the term paper done a day early instead of a day late. So if you have discovered any additional tech-niques that have helped you to make yourself do the things you know you should do—however weird, however odd those techniques may seem—I'd like to hear from you. My address:

> *Edwin C. Bliss*
> *El Rancho Loma Serena*
> *Mountain Ranch, California 95246*

Notes

STEP 1
Attitude Adjustment

1. Ogden Nash, *Verses from 1929 On*, from "Portrait of the Artist as a Prematurely Old Man." Copyright 1934 by Curtis Publishing Company. Original publication in *The Saturday Evening Post*.
2. Robert D. Abrahams, from "The Night They Burned Shanghai." © 1938 by Robert D. Abrahams. Reprinted by permission.
3. James Albery, "Epitaph Written for Himself," in *Homebook of Quotations*. New York: Dodd, Mead, 1964.

4. *Intellect*, November 1977, p. 185.
5. John W. Gardner, *Excellence*. New York: Harper & Row, 1961.
6. William James, *The Energies of Men*. New York: Longmans, Green & Co., 1911.

STEP 2
Develop a Game Plan

1. Albert Henry Smyth, ed. *The Writings of Benjamin Franklin*, vol. 5. New York: Macmillan, 1905, p. 437.
2. Ira Progoff, *At a Journal Workshop*. New York: Dialogue House, 1975, p. 290.
3. Donald M. Frame, ed. and trans. *Selections from the Essays of Montaigne*. Arlington Heights, Ill.: Harlan-Davidson Co., 1973.
4. Marvin R. Godfried and Michael Merbaum, "How to Control Yourself." *Psychology Today*, November 1973, p. 102.
5. Christian Cafarkis, *The Fabulous Onassis*. New York: William Morrow and Co., 1972.
6. Mack R. Douglas, *How to Make a Habit of Succeeding*. Grand Rapids, Michigan: Zondervan Books, 1972, p. 168.
7. Sid Caesar with Bill Davidson, *Where Have I Been?* New York: Crown Publishers, 1982, p. 235.
8. William Glasser, M.D. *Reality Therapy*. New York: Harper & Row, 1965, p. 39.
9. Richard Nelson Bolles, *What Color Is Your Parachute?* Berkeley, California: Ten Speed Press, 1982 edition, p. 64.
10. Benjamin Franklin, *The Autobiography and Other Writings*. New York: Signet, 1961, p. 99.

STEP 3
Overcome Fear of Failure

1. Gail Sheehy, *Pathfinders*. New York: Bantam Books, 1982, p. 112.
2. Abraham Maslow, *Eupsychian Management*. Homewood, Illinois: Richard D. Irwin, Inc., 1965, p. 7.
3. Roberto Assagioli, M.D. *The Act of Will*. New York: Viking Press, 1973, p. 81.
4. William James, *Varieties of Religious Experience*, Lecture 3. New York: Modern Library, 1936.
5. Harry Golden, *Only In America*. New York: Permabook, 1959, p. 304.
6. W. Timothy Gallwey, *The Inner Game of Tennis*. New York: Random House, 1974.
7. Bertrand Russell, *The Conquest of Happiness*. New York: Liveright Publishing Corp., 1930, p. 76.
8. Thomas Carlyle, *Sartor Resartus*. Darby, Pa.: Arden Library, 1981, p. 178.

STEP 4
Overcome Fear of Success

1. Abraham Maslow, *The Farther Reaches of Human Nature*. New York: Viking Press, 1971, p. 35.
2. Henry A. Murray, "American Icarus," from *Clinical Studies in Personality*. New York: Harper & Row, 1955. See also Michael Korda, *Success!* New York: Random House, 1977, p. 206.
3. Martha Friedman, *Overcoming the Fear of Success*. New York: Seaview Books, 1980, p. 136.
4. Laurence Peter, *The Peter Principle*. New York: William Morrow and Co., 1969.

5. Edgar Lee Masters, *Spoon River Anthology*. New York: Macmillan, 1915.

STEP 5
Raise Your Energy Level

1. Leonard Haimes, M.D., and Richard Tyson, M.D. *How to Triple Your Energy*. Chicago: Playboy Press, 1977, p. 90.
2. Laurence E. Morehouse and Leonard Gross, *Total Fitness*. New York: Simon & Schuster, 1975, p. 30.
3. Henry D. McIntosh, M.D. *Journal of the American Medical Association*, June 8, 1979, p. 2547.
4. James A. White, "Stand-Up Guys Raise Level of Discourse in Executive Suite." *Wall Street Journal*, October 21, 1982, p. 1.
5. Arthur E. Newbold III. *Wall Street Journal*, November 2, 1982, p. 27.
6. Laurence E. Morehouse and Leonard Gross, *Maximum Performance*. New York: Simon & Schuster, 1977, p. 80.
7. Herbert Benson, *The Relaxation Response*. New York: William Morrow and Co., 1975, p. 78.
8. *Consumer Reports* study, quoted in *The Harvard Medical School Health Letter Book*. New York: Warner Books, Inc., 1982, p. 224.
9. Peggy Mann, "Marijuana Alert III: Devastation of Personality." *Reader's Digest*, December 1981, p. 83.
10. *Encyclopaedia Britannica*, Fatigue, 15th edition (1974) 7:192.
11. William James, "The Energies of Men," from *Memories and Studies*. New York: Longmans, Green & Co., 1911.

STEP 6
Get Tough with Yourself

1. *Encyclopaedia Britannica*, "Exercise and Physical Conditioning," 15th edition (1974) 7:72.
2. William James, *Talks to Teachers*. New York: W. W. Norton and Co., 1958, p. 75.
3. Roberto Assagioli, M.D. *The Act of Will*. New York: Viking Press, 1973.
4. Boyd Barrett, *Strength of Will and How to Develop It*. New York: Richard R. Smith, Inc., 1931.
5. Napoleon Hill, *Think and Grow Rich*. New York: Fawcett Crest Books, 1963, p. 139.
6. Peter Drucker, *The Effective Executive*. New York: Harper & Row, 1966, p. 32.
7. Rudyard Kipling, from "If," *Rudyard Kipling's Verse*. Definitive ed. New York: Doubleday & Co., 1910.

STEP 7
Establish an Action Environment

1. *Success Unlimited*, September, 1977, p. 90.

STEP 8
Use the Reinforcement Principle

1. Robert L. Williams and James D. Long, *Toward a Self-Managed Life Style*. Boston: Houghton Mifflin Co., 1979, p. 171.
2. M. G. Perri and C. S. Richards, "An Investigation of Naturally Occurring Episodes of Self-Controlled Be-

haviors." *Journal of Counseling Psychology*, vol. 24, p. 178.

3. Albert Ellis and William J. Knaus, *Overcoming Procrastination*. New York: New American Library, 1977, p. 94. See also David Premack, "Reinforcement Theory," in *Nebraska Symposium on Motivation*. Lincoln, Nebraska: University of Nebraska Press, 1965.

STEP 9
Use Deliberate Delay

1. Mark Stein, *The T-Factor*. Chicago: Playboy Publications, 1977, p. 180.
2. Leonard Mosley, *Marshall: Hero for our Times*. New York: Hearst Books, 1982, p. 272.
3. Claude-Anne Lopez and Eugenia W. Herbert, *The Private Franklin*. New York: W. W. Norton & Co., 1975, p. 198.
4. Ross A. Webber, "The Art of Constructive Procrastination." *Wall Street Journal*, August 23, 1982, p. 16.
5. Mark Stein, *op. cit.*, p. 186.
6. Michael Doyle and David Straus, *How to Make Meetings Work*. Chicago: Playboy Press, 1976.
7. Alan Lakein, *How to Get Control of Your Time and Your Life*. New York: Peter H. Wyden, Inc., 1973, p. 186.

STEP 10
Manage Your Time

1. Mark Stein, *The T-Factor*. Chicago: Playboy Publications, 1977, p. 112.

2. Sydney J. Harris, *Winners and Losers*. New York: Argus Communications, 1973.

3. John F. Mee, "The Zeigarmik Effect." *Business Horizons* (June 1969), p. 53.

4. Robert I. Fitzhenry, ed. *Barnes and Noble Book of Quotations*. New York: Harper & Row, 1983, p. 303.

5. Gail Sheehy, *Passages*. New York: E. P. Dutton, 1976, p. 513.

STEP 11
Use Visible Reminders

1. Janette Rainwater, *You're in Charge!* Los Angeles: Peace Press, 1979, p. 96.

STEP 12
The Top Forty

1. David Riesman, *The Lonely Crowd: A Study of the Changing American Character*. New Haven: Yale University Press, 1950.

About the Author

ED BLISS has had a varied career as a newspaperman, editor, assistant to a senator, lobbyist, association executive and business consultant. Author of the popular *Getting Things Done*, he is a frequent speaker on time management, procrastination, and managerial effectiveness. A native of Salt Lake City, he received his bachelor's and master's degrees from the University of Utah and now lives in Mountain Ranch, California.

Bantam Guides to Better English Usage

- [ ] **25552 THE BANTAM CONCISE HANDBOOK OF ENGLISH** $3.95

- [ ] **23933 THE BANTAM INSTANT SPELLING HANDBOOK** $3.95

- [ ] **27086 THE BANTAM BOOK OF CORRECT LETTER WRITING** $4.50

- [ ] **27041 BUSINESS WRITING HANDBOOK** $4.50

- [ ] **26376 WRITER'S SURVIVAL MANUAL** $4.50

- [ ] **27046 WRITING & RESEARCHING TERM PAPERS** $3.95